ADVOCATES
& ENEMIES

ADVOCATES & ENEMIES

How to build practical strategies to influence your stakeholders

COLIN GAUTREY

the gautrey group

www.thegautreygroup.com

Dedication

To my children...

Sarah, who found strength, gritty resolve and a new home arise from the devastation of the Japanese earthquake this year,

Luci, who I think this year has found her passion and learnt that great rewards follow determination and hard work,

and

James, who is showing early signs of a quirky sense of humour, a love of literature, and the spark of ambition to be an author.

Whatever the future holds in store for them, my sincere wish is that they find happiness, whatever that means to them.

Acknowledgements

First and foremost, to all those thousands of great people who have honoured me with their time and a desire to learn. I may have helped you, but you have also helped me and been the inspiration for this work.

Secondly, to everyone I engage with in my network. Your challenge, friendship and support are very much appreciated.

And last but by no means least, to my two close colleagues, David Wilson and Maureen Atkins. Without their ability to respond with lightning speed to the deluge of brainwaves, new models, alternative ideas and drafts – well, I don't know what I would have done. Thank you for your challenge, support and friendship.

Contents

Foreword

In October 2010, Colin and I were having lunch at Grand Central Terminal, NYC's famous train station. As we looked down on the main concourse, I marveled at the way so many millions of people were able to navigate from one side of the hall to the other without bumping into each other. They come from every different angle seeking many different exits so they can go about their day. While some look harried in the rush towards their destination, others have a copy of *USA Today* in one hand and a coffee in the other as they amble calmly across the hall. What none of them seem to be doing is thinking about how they are moving through the crowd — they seem to be on auto-pilot, despite the huge complexity of the physical task of avoiding knocking people over, or being trampled by others.

And then I made the comparison with corporate life. At work we are all coming from somewhere, and we are all going someplace. Yes, and most of us are in a rush too. And as we move forward, we have to navigate a safe path through the crowds of other ambitious people whom we work with. But there the analogy to Grand Central starts to falter. When you look at most organizations, people keep bumping into each other. They knock others over and are knocked over themselves. The groceries lie scattered across the floor and people trample on others' livelihoods. Why is this? How can people dance so nimbly across a busy rail station but not get through a day at work without going wrong?

Imagine what would happen if you put a blindfold on someone and asked them to rush from one side of Grand Central to the other. What you have done is given them a result to achieve but removed the ability for them to see what is going on around them – to see what others are doing and how they are moving. You have removed their ability to sense what's going on, to make predictions about where others will be within a few more steps, and thus prevented them from moving safely from one side of the concourse to the other.

And here I think lies the clue. At work people get their targets, they get focused on what they have to achieve and how they are going to do that, but they look down at their feet and are probably only aware of their most immediate neighbors. Few people are able to look up and out at the bigger world. If they did that, they would notice other big obstacles, but also other big opportunities to help them to navigate safely to their destination. Many people at work are trying to get from A to B with their eyes closed, and that can hurt them and also cause harm to others.

The next day, we did our workshop for a group of senior executives from Corporate America. It was fascinating to see how Colin was able to open their eyes in just a few hours.

Drawing on his research and experience, he was able to help them to quickly figure out their best route to overcome their challenges and achieve their goals. Helping them to look up and out at the bigger picture, but without wasting time worrying about the small stuff, or insisting they first understand the theory. Colin's practical ideas, concepts and tools do the job extremely well.

At times, I think we all get stuck in our ways; we get into the detail and miss the bigger picture. That is, I suppose, a natural part of life. When we realize this, or it is pointed out to us, it becomes obvious that something needs to change. We need to take a different approach and so our search for solutions and new ways begins. And that search becomes more and more complicated with every step forward in technology. It's amazing how many clever people are out there, who have all the right theories and yet seem to have lost a vital ingredient. Trying to seduce you with their cleverness, they have missed the desperate need for simplicity.

And that's what I am so pleased to see in this book. Colin is very engaging in his workshops and it is great to see the way he has captured his energy and enthusiasm, along with his simple techniques, in such a concise book. I think you're going to enjoy this and I hope it brings you even greater success in the future.

Dr. Gary Ranker
New York City, August 2011

Author's Preface

The title of this book conjures up dramatic scenes. Intrigue, plots and counter plots reminiscent of a John Grisham bestseller. Or maybe it calls to mind Michael Douglas' epic portrayal of Gordon Gekko in the 1987 blockbuster *Wall Street.* Is this relevant to your work? Well, I hope it's not that extreme. Whatever your position in the world of work, I firmly believe that this book will help you to further your ambition and success.

Why? Because this is a book about taking decisive action to further your goals – whatever they may be. The title is there to give the initial spark to your motivation to pause – not for long – so you can go faster. The content will stimulate you to think differently about your work. It will also provoke you into action. Without action you're unlikely to achieve anything meaningful. It will not bring out the Gekko megalomaniac in you. Instead, it will inspire you to take authentic action with full regard not only for other people's agendas, but also for other people's wellbeing.

Over the years, I have been fortunate to work with highly talented people. People who are recognised by their organisations as being the best – destined for higher roles, bigger challenges, and certainly worth looking after and retaining. Yet so many struggled with the onslaught – the relentless pressure for results. The consequence was that they often missed a simple and highly critical element of their work. When the pressure came on, they worked harder not smarter.

This is where I came in. Unencumbered by the organisational politics and independent of the action, I was able to get them to pause, to think and then to go faster. The additional results they achieved were remarkable. Not only did they easily surpass expectations (their own and their bosses), but they were also able to stretch their thinking, aspire to greater things and also go home at night to their families relaxed and ready to switch off.

It was during this work that I was first introduced to the idea of stakeholder management. Not the complex multiple-dimensional approach used by engineers and government departments, but a simple and pragmatic way of mapping out the territory in order to get a clear picture of what needed to happen to achieve the result. Over the years, I have helped thousands to apply it, and in the process I have learned about the key ingredients and gradually refined it into what I now call the *Stakeholder Influence Process*. A process so simple it can be learned within an hour. It is a process so effective that once you've learned how to use it and seen the results it can give you – you will want to keep using it for as long as you have an ambition to influence others.

My most sincere wish right now is that this little book causes you to pause (just for a moment), so you can then go faster!

Colin Gautrey
London, July 2011

CHAPTER ONE

Simple Process, Stunning Results

Mark opened his notebook and the evidence lay at the back on a few pieces of paper. Not much more than a few lines and scribbled names. But it was enough, we both knew the code. Here was the evidence that Mark was still applying the *Stakeholder Influence Process*. Five years after I first worked with him, it had become an integral part of his *modus operandi*.

Originally, I was asked to work with Mark to help him to develop his approach to gaining stakeholder buy-in. As a senior executive, he had evolved his own way of doing things, like we all do. However, in a complex and fast moving global business, it had been recognised that this was not as effective as it needed to be. So we designed a programme of six-hour-long remote coaching sessions.

As we started working together, I insisted that we agree on a specific goal that we could use as focus for our discussions – one that he and his organisation would gain great benefit from when realised. His top priority right then was bringing consistency (and savings) to the way they procured services across the Asia Pacific region. We got to work.

In one of our sessions, I showed him how to take a practical and strategic approach to engaging with his stakeholders. We mapped out his stakeholders, analysed them and discussed their agendas, issues and his relationship with them. From that, he quickly worked out a strategy for gaining their buy-in. Simple actions which had not occurred to him before. None of them involved the deployment of new skills. Nor did they require him to go into battle, chase conflict or force people to agree with him. All that was needed was an effective way of thinking it through and tapping into his existing knowledge and skill. All this happened in a single-hour-long telephone call.

Within six months of starting work with Mark, he had succeeded in getting his procurement strategy signed off by the APAC executive board. This was projected to yield first-year savings of over $28 million. He cited the stakeholder management approach as being critical in gaining the support he needed, overcoming strong opposition, and helping him to land the result. A $28 million result!

Of course, there was much more to achieving the result than a little bit of stakeholder management. He had to deploy high levels of intelligence, skill, logic, persuasion, etc. However, what it did do was ensure that he got focused on the people that mattered most, was able to think through his approach and realise the critical arguments which he needed to address in order to get his result. The evidence at the back of his notebook showed that it has remained an approach central to all of his important work today – and it took just an hour to learn!

Mark is just one of many examples I could have given of how people at all levels have benefited from the ideas, concepts and techniques contained in this book. Over the last eight or so years, I have worked with thousands of people at all levels and in many countries. Almost without exception, the response has been extremely positive. They have found that this simple approach helps them to focus on the important considerations among their stakeholders.

And if it can work for Mark, it can start to work for you – in less than an hour!

What is the Stakeholder Influence Process?

The *Stakeholder Influence Process* is a sequence of steps which will help you work out what you need to do to achieve your goals when they are reliant on the agreement of other powerful people. It provides a simple framework to think through the situation you wish to influence, your goal or the project you are managing. It will help you to figure out who is onside and who may be out to get you.

From that you can start to develop your strategy to accomplish your goal. This will probably involve engaging with people you may have overlooked before. Before starting the process, you may have considered them to be minor players or not even interested. Some of them may not be interested in what you are doing, but the *Stakeholder Influence Process* may uncover opportunities to collaborate for mutual benefit, or perhaps simply bring their attention to all that they could gain from your work. If they are powerful people in your organisation, this alone could help you to reach your goal.

This simple process is shown on the next page.

Don't let the simplicity distract you. Within each step are some fairly profound principles which add significantly to the potential of the process. Principles established through years of practical application in a wide variety of situations. These will be explored in later chapters. Right now, I want to stress that this process is iterative. You can speed through the process once and get new actions popping out all over the place. Then you can come back and do it again and go a little deeper. Each time you do this, there will be more things you can think about, more actions you can develop, and more progress you can make.

The *Stakeholder Influence Process* is not about complex theories of human behaviour. Instead, it will focus on simple questions like...

- What does each stakeholder want to achieve?
- Why have you positioned them there?
- What's the history?

Exploring the answers to these questions, and more, around a simple framework will quickly help you to discover the key moves you need to make. Usually, these moves can be achieved with your current skills. Most people don't need

The Stakeholder Influence Process

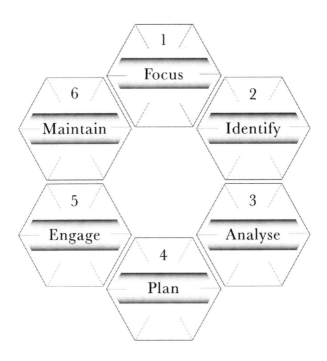

Step 1 – **Focus**: Assess your priorities and focus your Influencing Goal.

Step 2 – **Identify**: Work out which stakeholders can have the biggest impact.

Step 3 – **Analyse**: Map the position of each stakeholder.

Step 4 – **Plan**: Decide your strategy for increasing buy-in.

Step 5 – **Engage**: Adapt your approach to influence your stakeholders.

Step 6 – **Maintain**: Keep the momentum going with regular reviews.

to develop new skills. Often it is simply a question of applying existing skills in different ways or with a different focus. Sometimes you just need to do what you have been avoiding for far too long, and the *Stakeholder Influence Process* will help you to see that and then get on with it!

To be totally frank, the key here is in gaining the awareness of what you need to do. There is no deep psychology, just a simple process which demands crisp answers to basic questions. And it gets results – time and time again.

And to continue being frank, this process is not suitable for everyone. To get maximum value out of this approach, you probably need to be able to tick most of the following...

☐ You recognise that influence is a key part of your job.

☐ You need to gain the support of a variety of different people.

☐ Your goal has natural opposition or

☐ Many different opinions exist about what the right answer is.

☐ You want to become more influential.

☐ You are very busy at work.

☐ You are able to just give it a go.

The most important item on the list above is the last one. Without this you are probably going nowhere. I cannot think of a single individual who has not benefitted after making the effort of putting pen to paper and following the process. And it doesn't take much effort or time to make real progress.

How will you benefit?

If you give it a half decent go, you will quickly start to notch up the benefits. Over the years, I have seen people achieve remarkable advances in a very short space of time in so many different areas. For example, clients have been able to...

- Focus their time on what will make the biggest difference to their success.
- Reduce the risks of failure and be more prepared if those risks start to materialise.
- Dramatically increase buy-in, getting more people to actively support their work.
- Deliver their projects in record time, with fewer problems and enhanced benefit realisation.
- Pull out of the detail so they could take a more strategic view.
- Achieve much more with much less.
- Become more confident, assured and less stressed.
- Attract the attention of the talent spotters at the top of their organisation.
- Move forward their career, sometimes several steps at a time.

The *Stakeholder Influence Process* is also useful in a very wide range of pursuits. Over the last eight years, I have seen it being successfully used by clients who are...

- Delivering programmes and projects (big and small)
- Launching new products
- Starting businesses
- Managing crises
- Implementing change initiatives
- Turning around failing businesses
- Accelerating their careers
- Managing suppliers
- Introducing new systems

Basically, anything you need to achieve, which requires determined effort over a period of time and involves lots of people, is likely to be aided significantly by the *Stakeholder Influence Process*. Recently, I saw one delegate on a workshop use it during the coffee break to develop a strategy for improving the relationship she had with her mother-in-law!

While all of the above sound great, it needs to be recognised that the *Stakeholder Influence Process* is not going to immediately solve all of your problems. What it will do is help you to identify the actions you need to take in order to start making progress on your problems. You still have to take responsibility and implement the actions. You still need to exercise skill, persistence and creativity in arriving at the solution. Without the *Stakeholder Influence Process*, people often struggle to make sense of what is going on. They get stuck in the detail, buffeted by the problems and issues, and are unable to make sense of what is happening to them (or their project). This process is the beginning of end for these problems.

Another factor which needs to be stressed is that for some readers the benefit will be unexpected and, at least in the short term, a little uncomfortable and stressful. Occasionally, when I have coached people with this process, they have realised that the goal they are striving for is simply not going to happen. Maybe the powerful forces moving against them are simply too much, the opposition too strong, or the project they are working on was ill-conceived and really should not be implemented. Going through the process can become a little emotional, but at the end of the day there is little point working on something that is doomed. Eventually, the process gave them the confidence and the thinking to engage their stakeholders in healthy and objective debate and bring forward the decision to cancel their project. Without doubt, these decisions were tough. However, what these individuals managed to avoid was many hours of agony and wasted time, effort and money.

Those who had the courage of their convictions benefited greatly in the long run because their organisations realised the value that they brought. Although their projects may have been cancelled, they quickly became eagerly sought after for other critical initiatives. In many ways, what they had discovered is the power that often comes from showing such commitment to the organisation that they were even willing to stake their own future on finding the right solution for the organisation. A rare quality indeed!

However, these sorts of unexpected benefits are very much in the minority. Most people are able to protect their projects from sabotage, conflicting priorities and agendas.

Basically, they move their work forward with much more support and safety than their competition – simply by applying the *Stakeholder Influence Process*.

There are no magic pills, panaceas or quick fixes here. But what this approach does do is help you to quickly find the action which needs to be taken, the arguments or debates which need to be conducted, so that you can move forward and overcome any opposition which may be waiting to thwart your endeavours.

How can you apply this in less than an hour?

My basic assumption is that you haven't got much free time and you recognise the importance of taking a more strategic approach to managing your stakeholders. If this applies to you, go straight to *Chapter Thirteen*; read it, do the exercises, prioritise your actions and you're on your way! And you should be able to achieve that in an hour.

Of course, you can always spend more time, but please try to focus on taking action as quickly as possible. Then, when you've taken some action, come back to the process again and do some more thinking; read a little more, go a little deeper and you will quickly develop a robust approach to making things happen.

All of the other chapters provide additional depth to the process and deal with other critical background subjects which I have found to be of immense value as people develop their practise. Naturally, you can skip and skim through these, but make sure to come back at some point in order to fill in the gaps – the ideas in these chapters can really make a big difference to your performance.

So, focus on *Chapter Thirteen* to get going fast. It provides a brief overview which anyone with a reasonable amount of common sense and experience can get moving with – fast. If you follow my suggestion here, within a very short space of time the *Stakeholder Influence Process* will embed itself into your *modus operandi* – just like it did with Mark.

The most important concept here is action. This process works. It is being used by project managers, marketing managers, IT specialists, lawyers and executives at every level in some of the biggest corporations in the world. If it can work for them, it can work for you.

So just do it, okay?

Hold on just a moment before you dive into *Chapter Thirteen*. Often I find that the biggest obstacle to effective influence is remembering to do what you've learned (or indeed remembered). With such a busy life, it is difficult at the best of times remembering to do what you know you should be doing, particularly when you have lots of people putting you under pressure for all manner of things.

So you might like to find a way of keeping this present in your mind, a way of being reminded that it's a smart idea to do it. One way of doing this, which I would encourage you to do, is to follow **The Influence Blog.** The purpose of this blog is to give followers a once-a-week insight or idea about how to become more influential. When it drops into your inbox, it will be a good reminder for you, and yet another way of improving your practise while also reminding you to get your stakeholder plan out again.

Okay, blatant but well intentioned self-promotion over, move to *Chapter Thirteen* now.

The Influence Blog

Weekly insights helping followers to become more influential, enhance their results and move forward their careers

www.advocatesandenemies.com/blog

CHAPTER TWO

Step 1: Focus
Assess your priorities and focus your Influencing Goal

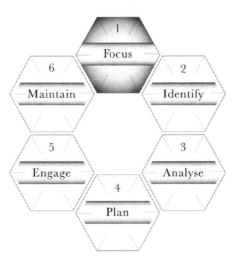

Unless you know exactly what you are shooting for, you will lose ground, miss opportunities and struggle to get buy-in. If you are clear, you'll move much faster, save time and get even better results. You need to get focused not only on your end goal, but also on what you need to influence to get there. The first step in the *Stakeholder Influence Process* is to clarify what you want to focus on.

Action

Pause to consider all of the important things which are going on in your life/work at the moment.

Think about...

- What targets and projects have you got at work this year?
- What are your personal goals for this year? Next year?
- Where are you hoping to take your career?
- Are you facing particular difficulties or issues at work (or at home) at present which you'd like to resolve?
- What do you want to achieve in the next couple of years?
- What goals are there beyond the ones right in front of you?

This is a warm-up exercise to get your thoughts moving, and considering your bigger picture. In a moment, you can start to work on developing the focus. This action can be very useful in making sure you've not missed anything critical. If you've already done this general thinking, no problem, just move on to the next action. Otherwise, put the book down and muse a short while. Pen and paper would be quite useful here too!

Once you've taken a little time to reflect on this, you need to settle on one or two topics which you can use this book to move forward on. Ideally, you're looking for a goal which…

- Is of critical importance to you.
- Can motivate you – or even get you really excited!
- Will stretch your skill set and involve a fair degree of influencing to make it happen.
- Ranks high in your list of priorities overall when deciding where to spend your time and energy.

Bear in mind that the goal you want to move forward could be a shared goal – it doesn't have to be something which is only important to you. In fact, if it is a goal shared by a team or a few of your peers, this will make it even better to work on with the *Stakeholder Influence Process* because you can all share, learn and play your part in realising the objective.

You may also decide to work on somebody else's goal. By that, I mean that you may not have formal responsibility for it; but if you feel strongly that something needs to happen, you could choose to make it your business to push it forward. But before you rush off poking your nose into other people's business, stop to consider how your action may be perceived – not only by the person who should be pushing forward on that goal, but also by the stakeholders who are connected with it. Some may wonder about your motives, so think about doing some careful positioning before you go too far, too fast. But at the end of the day, sometimes acts like these are necessary!

Suggestion

If your goal is also important to your partner and family, this could be great as they become a stakeholder too!

Action

Review your notes from the deliberations above and pick one goal you'd like to focus on. Make a note of it in the space below.

I'm not going to patronise you by talking about SMART goals and things like that, but it is important that in your own mind – or even on paper – you are able to be very clear about what success looks like. The clearer you can be, the better. Unless you get specific, you may simply have some aims. Nothing wrong with that; but if you want to move faster, get clearer.

Suggestion

If you cannot be clear with yourself, how will anyone else understand what you want?

This activity should have helped to review and focus what you want to achieve; however, in this process, you need to think in terms of what you have to influence in order to achieve your goal – for this reason, I use the term *Influencing Goal.*

Here's a working definition of influence which I find practical for the *Stakeholder Influence Process*...

Definition

Influence: Getting people to willingly act, think or feel differently.

There are a couple of elements of this definition which are worth exploring briefly. Firstly, I'm using the word "willingly" here because this will help you to focus on getting longer-term buy-in. You can get someone to do something by simply *telling* them to do it – particularly easy if they happen to report to you! The fact that they would rather not do it does not mean that they wouldn't do it. But turn your back for a moment and they may go back to what they were doing before. Similarly, you could *ask* them to do something and they would do it. Without adding in a little motivation to get them to want to do it, they may go back to doing what they were doing before the moment you turn away. Of course, they may still revert to their previous behaviour, but it is much less likely if you have been diligent in your motivational influencing. So including "willingly" in my definition will hopefully help you to stay focused on getting them to really want to do what you want them to do.

Secondly, it is often the case that we need to move hearts and minds; therefore, we want to work towards getting people to feel differently. A common example of this is getting them to be positive about a forthcoming change in procedures or systems. Similarly, on occasion, the most important thing for us is to get people thinking a little different. One example of this would be influencing a group of sales people to think about involving the marketing team at the right stage of the sales process. You might not need them to do something different on every occasion, just make sure that they think it and, therefore, make a clear decision about the need to involve marketing in the case in hand.

You will also notice that my definition includes a change of some sort. Strictly speaking, this is not always the case. Sometimes, it is necessary to ensure that your stakeholders continue acting/thinking or feeling in a particular way. However, most of the time we end up working on creating a change of some sort. Let's not get too worried about semantics.

The final point is that this definition refers to "people". The reason for this is that the *Stakeholder Influence Process* will generate maximum benefit when it is focussed on helping you to build strategies to move the masses, rather than just individuals. It can be useful with individuals (particularly if they are very senior people, in which case you will need to create a campaign of action to get them to endorse your new idea), but this is not the usual use.

With this in mind, the next question to answer is...

> What do you want/need to influence to dramatically improve your progress towards your chosen goal?

When you can answer this, you should discover where you need to direct your influence, and also your application of the *Stakeholder Influence Process*. This is what I refer to as your *Influencing Goal* in the rest of the book. You may wonder about the difference between a "goal" and an "influencing goal". The latter makes sure to put the focus on how you need to move people in order to achieve the former. Depending on how you have defined your main goal, they could be the same.

For instance, if your main goal is to "achieve sales revenue of $650k", your *Influencing Goal* right now might be to "get the Marketing Board to sign off my sales strategy". This focuses on people doing something different – signing off your strategy. Alternatively, if your main goal right now is that "The board will sign off my marketing budget of $250k", this is both a goal and also your *Influencing Goal.* Most of the time you will need to influence quite a few different things to get your budget, so you can settle on an *Influencing Goal* which is the most critical thing you need to influence right now to accelerate you towards the sign-off. Still confused? Don't worry, just move on. The difference will soon become clear once you've been through the process a few times.

Influencing Goals which tend to work best in this process are the ones which...

- ✓ Are a top priority for you in your work.
- ✓ Require many people to think, feel or act differently.
- ✓ Need to overcome tough opposition from others.
- ✓ Require a plan of action over several months.
- ✓ Are important to other people as well.

Put another way, an *Influencing Goal* that is rarely suitable is one that...

x   Only needs one person to say yes.
x   Could be achieved in one meeting.
x   Really belongs to someone else.
x   Has an easily understandable logic which everyone can agree to.
x   Is more of a wish than a key part of your life or work.

Of course, if the one person you need to say "yes" is inaccessible to you because they are too high in the organisation, this could be very applicable to this process because you may need to find lots of others (stakeholders) who could influence on your behalf or open up the opportunity for you to speak to them.

Action

With your priority goal in mind, think about what you need to influence (or whom). Develop a list of the different things which need to change – *Influencing Goals.*

Consider...
•   What could you change which will have a big positive impact on your success? (Could, not can – this is not the stage to apply your talent for realism!)

- What are the major obstacles standing in your way?
- Do others hold particular attitudes which stand in your way or are working against you?

Any project or goal that you are working on is likely to contain many things which you need to influence. The skill here is in selecting the one which is most important now. You cannot work on dozens of goals all at the same time and expect to be focused!

Here are some examples of *Influencing Goals* my clients have chosen to focus their stakeholder management...

1. Achieve planning committee approval for the new building in Regents Street.
2. Increase requests for advice from internal clients fivefold by the end of this year.
3. Remove Compliance Department's opposition to our new marketing strategy.
4. Gain positive feedback from at least six directors within the next four months.
5. Become widely recognised as Samantha's successor.
6. Increase Market Share to 12% next year.
7. Be appointed chair of the Networking Group at the next Annual General Meeting.
8. Secure $250k additional funding for my product line.

9. Get Jerry's buy-in to my proposal before the next board meeting.

10. Achieve a clear go/no go decision at the next Steering Committee meeting in July.

As you can see, there is a wide variety here. Most of them make it clear who has to be influenced, although some are implied. Nearly all require a campaign of action over a period of time and the agreement of more than one person.

Goal six is an interesting one because it implies that the market needs to be influenced and is also a high-level goal. In order to achieve that influence, the individual I was working with broke it down into a series of different *Influencing Goals.* The marketing department needed to be persuaded to sign off the development strategy; the board needed to be convinced to allocate enough advertising budget, etc. So under this big goal was a series of *Influencing Goals.*

The important thing to note here is that you need to select an *Influencing Goal* which is at a level that is helpful to you right now. Sometimes, people need to move either down in scale or nearer in time to get moving. It is impossible to say which is right for you, but what I can assure is that most people discover the right level of goal within a few iterations of the process. If you're focusing too high, Step 6: Maintain should flush it out and you'll then be able to adjust your focus in a more practical way.

Action

Take your list of potential *Influencing Goals* and choose one that you can focus on now. Write it down in the space below.

Consider – which one is...

...the most exciting?

...causing the most stress?

...going to help you to take the biggest step forward?

...going to make lots of other goals easier?

...the most motivational?

Of course, you can use the *Stakeholder Influence Process* for more than one of your goals, but make sure to consider them separately to avoid getting mixed up. And definitely use a different stakeholder map in Step 3.

A final piece of thinking in this step, which could be very helpful, is how you will know you have achieved the desired influence. For many of the example *Influencing Goals* I gave earlier it is clear from the wording – the board either signed off the proposal or they didn't. But ones like becoming recognised as Samantha's successor are a little more difficult. How would you know you are recognised as a successor? The more clarity you get, the more progress you will make. So if this applies to you, see if you can come up with some evidence criteria for your goal similar to this...

Example

Influencing Goal: Become widely recognised as Samantha's successor: as evidenced by...

- Without prompting, team colleagues refer questions to me when Sam's not around.
- Sam's boss calls me when he can't get an answer from Sam.
- I am formally on the succession plan.
- Sam tells me that I'm her preferred successor.
- I get a place on the new Leadership Development Program.
- Cherry tells me it's obvious I'm in line for the top job.
- I am asked to stand in for Sam at the next quarterly committee meeting.

Suggestion

Although clarity is important, don't let the lack of it delay you too much before taking some action!

Over the years, I have found this to be one of the most important steps in the process where people can lose ground and benefit by trying to apply the *Stakeholder Influence Process* to unhelpful goals and challenges. Of course, this is not to say that the goals in themselves are not useful to strive for; it is simply that they are difficult to use as a focus for your influencing work.

The time and effort that you devote to clarifying your *Influencing Goal* will be well rewarded. I remember one director I was coaching who paused to consider what he needed to influence in order to achieve his goal. He soon became clear and went off to engage a stakeholder who was against his ideas. Later, he reported back that the stakeholder had easily agreed when he was given a clear request. Apparently, he had been fantasising about lots of things my client wanted which were actually untrue. Assumptions have a lot to answer for!

CHAPTER THREE

Exploring Organisational Power and Influence

When individuals make decisions about what they should do, how they should change, one of the (often unconscious) influencers is the presence of powerful people who could help or hinder them. Understanding how power affects decisions will help you to explore short cuts to creating the effect you need.

Many organisations function in complex ways, which make them very difficult to understand. Complexity grows with size, geographic spread and business diversity. The arrival of matrix structures and cross functional working has made organisations more integrated and nimble, but at the same time has added another layer of complexity.

In practical terms, what successful people need to get to grips with is the complexity of the decision-making processes – the formal, the informal and the often obtuse and irrational. To succeed with your *Influencing Goal*, you often need to get not only the organisation to buy in, but also the individuals right the way down the food chain – without whom implementation of your big idea could be somewhat sporadic.

Once you can work out why people do some things and not others, you will start to discover easier routes to getting things done. Whom to involve, whom you can ignore, which buttons to press and levers to pull. Trouble is that there is no rule book as these things tend to emerge within the culture of the organisation rather than be visible. Of course, there will be a sign-off process, but usually these are just rubber stamping exercises – the decision has already been made within the social fabric of the organisation.

And the quickest route to deciphering all of this is to learn about power. Once you see what power is and how it works, you will then be able to start to decode the way the business operates and realise the steps you need to take in order to make things happen.

The Components of Power

Power is not complicated – it is simple. The concept is regularly spoken of, but rarely understood at a practical level. Jeffrey Pfeffer (author of *Managing with Power*) usually defines it as...

Definition

Power: The capability to create influence.

In the last chapter, I used the following definition of influence...

Definition

Influence: Getting people to willingly act, think or feel differently.

The combination of these definitions covers a multitude of skills, tactics and assets (see below). What I've found is that most people focus on skills and tactics when they seek influence and fail to recognise the potency of the assets – many of which need to exist as the foundation of skills and tactics. I usually refer to these assets as the shortcuts to influence, and hopefully you'll soon see why. The distinction between skills, assets and tactics are easily illustrated.

Imagine you have a big bag of money – a particularly potent asset. You may be pretty good at drawing attention to your asset, perhaps you have a qualification in money bag shaking

– a useful skill indeed. Now when you come and wave it under my nose, that could be a very powerful tactic – provided of course that I am interested (i.e. I want some more) and cannot more easily acquire it from someone else!

The Components of Power

Assets
Position or Role
Network of Contacts
Physical
  Characteristics e.g.
  height
Knowledge,
  experience
Qualifications
Reputation
Access to information
Revenue or profit
  streams
Headcount, resources

Skills
Communication and
  persuasion
Assertiveness
Motivating and inspiring
Building rapport and trust
Charming and being
  likeable
Making use of assets

Tactics
Any specific exercise of
  skill

Practical Implications

Thinking about power in this way yields a number of interesting and useful ideas.

- You can achieve influence without using your skills or tactics – provided that people know you have the asset and want a slice of it – or want to avoid it!
- The potency of different types of assets can vary depending on supply and demand. Imagine a *"fist full of dollars"* – Zimbabwean dollars have rather less capability to influence than US dollars – well for most of us!
- Many people fantasise and make assumptions about your assets, particularly if they are of the more obscure or intangible variety – like relationships.
- People without valuable assets have to use lots of skills and tactics to gain influence – the office politician perhaps?
- Assets can be divided between different people and, of course, they can combine the power of their assets too.
- You can also lose your assets, spend them, invest them or suddenly have their value drop like a stone.

The distinctions between assets and skills are not pure, nor are they usually easy to categorise. For instance, some assets only have influence when they are used, such as the voice. This is a physical asset, honed into a skill, but is rarely influential unless you exercise it (in fact, it's a good example of a skill reliant on an asset used tactically). The classification is less important than the practical implications of thinking about power in this way.

Action

Pause for a moment and consider your own power. Why do people do what you want them to do? What skills and assets do you have which make you powerful?

Action

What about the people around you – what makes them powerful? Why do people do what they want them to do? Is it their stunning good looks, connection with the CEO or maybe their awesome reputation?

Thinking about power can show up some surprises – people whom you think are powerless or powerful are not necessarily always what you think they are. I recall one CEO many years ago complaining to me that he felt powerless to get his directors to do what he wanted them to do. They all agreed in the board meetings what should happen, then went back to their work and ignored the agreement.

Similarly, often junior people have much more ability to help or hinder than you think. The usual example is the secretary who has control of who gets in to see the boss. Alternatively, it could be the old hand who knows exactly how the organisation works and can pretty much do whatever they like because the organisation cannot risk losing their depth of knowledge, and having them onside could be the critical determinant of achieving your result – because they know exactly how to solve your road blocks.

Group/Organisational Power

You will probably have noticed that much of the phrasing above suggests personal ownership of assets or skills. This is true; however, the same also applies to groups of individuals, or even whole organisations. The combined effect of their individual assets and skills can become far more than the sum of their parts. This is what we usually refer to as group or organisational power. Common statements we hear about power include...

> "Marketing has the power to push that
> one through."
>
> "How come Sales always seem to get
> what they want?"

Although much of this is related to the combined individual assets and skills, that is not the whole story. To a large extent, the sort of assets and skills which are valued within an organisation are determined by the strategy the board or executives set in response to the external environment and shareholder expectations.

Put simply, if the directors recognise that market share is going to be squeezed, they'll turn the pressure up on the marketers to grab as much share as possible. Therefore, all eyes turn to those who are capable of growing the business top-line – and budgets are usually made available. Alternatively, they may take the approach that they have to batten down the hatches and cut costs to retain the profit margins – in which case, those who are in command of the numbers, financial experts, performance analysts and budget setters grow in power. This illustrates the point above about supply and demand.

In the context of the *Stakeholder Influence Process*, it is vitally important that you understand which of these powerful groups could have an interest in what you are doing (either positive or negative).

Formal and Informal Power

Another distinction that needs to be drawn is the difference between the power that is formally distributed around the organisation and that which is acquired by individuals (very similar to personal power).

With a business, shareholders provide the executive team with a big bag of money, some ideas about the sort of business they want to create and an indication of what return on investment they need. The team then decide their strategy to deliver the return and set about organising and managing the business. They create the departments they need, allocate money to them and recruit people to head them up. They give these heads the authority to make things happen within their departments. Each budget is then subdivided again to create teams and they then get on with the business. Of course, this is oversimplified, but it shows the basic principles of how the organisation formally starts to spread the power around the people and functions to get things moving.

Public sector and not-for-profit organisations operate in the same way, except that the key power asset driving the structure is likely to be the mandate and authority to act with money being a secondary consideration (I'll side step the debate about whether or not this should be the case, okay – that's just how it tends to work).

As the business matures, it will realise it needs to put in place some checks and balances. It therefore recruits a compliance manager and bestows upon him/her a remit to make sure that everyone is compliant; and if not, the power to force compliance. Again, this is a simple example of how power is formally created for the good of the business. Of course, this is not always as controlled by the top executives as they may like to think. I'm sure most people have witnessed "empire builders" collecting more and more departmental responsibilities. This is still an example of formal power.

However, this is very different from the informal power which usually takes the form of skills, capabilities and personalities. Experience and reputation also fall into this informal category. Curiously, qualifications are a formal asset usually regarded as an informal or personal asset, largely because it is given by a different organisation, so it has a high degree of independence from the current employer or place where the individual is working.

The reason for drawing your attention to this is that if you want to become powerful, remember that formal assets are generally given to people and/or can be taken away again; whereas informal assets are built and owned by the individuals and placed at the disposal of the organisation. The point to note is that if you want to build a solid power base, make sure that you build formal as well as informal assets as a sound investment in your future success.

Power and Stakeholders

The bottom line here is that it is your powerful stakeholders whom you need to start paying attention to, particularly if you are ambitious and want to make great things happen. These are the people who can stop your project dead in its tracks or help you to be first past the post.

Within the organisation, power will be ebbing and flowing. Battles will be waged, wars won and peace made. The competition for power (like it or not) is raging in most organisations, often just below the surface. On the top of this comes the myriad of projects and initiatives supported and challenged with the personal motives foremost in the mind of many of the contenders. All may not be as it seems.

Example

I recall one lady I was coaching who was proudly presenting her project plans to me. It involved restructuring the London business (£1bn gross revenue).

Q: Who is the most powerful person in the company?
A: Sales Director.
Q: What makes him powerful?
A: He brings in 75% of the revenue.
Q: What impact will your change have?
A: Ah, um, we're planning to split up his division.
Q: Have you got him bought in?
A: Oh dear.

After much expense, the project died. Three years later, the business restructured without problem by promoting the Sales Director to CEO. Early recognition of the potential impact your plans may have on the power of key players can help you to save time, money, effort and goodwill. It can also help you to realise where you should really be focusing your influence!

It is here that the keys to success lie. Irrespective of the sound logic that your goal or project has, if it is impacting the power bases of senior people in the organisation, you absolutely must take this into account.

CHAPTER FOUR

Step 2: Identify
Work out which stakeholders can have the biggest impact

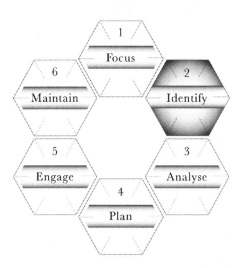

To achieve your goals and influence effectively, it is vital to focus your energy on those who can have the greatest ability to help or hinder. Without this focus, people tend to work on those who are nearest, best known or most convenient rather than those whom they should be influencing.

The title "Stakeholder" has been gaining popularity over the last few years. Its traditional use refers to large groups of people, often with a somewhat nebulous, yet real existence – the media, the public and shareholders are often what's being referred to. As such, stakeholders used to be the chief concern of high level boards and committees. However, the shift in popular usage is happening because of the realisation that the ideas used at a high level to manage these groups can apply just as well to more humble pursuits – the sort of projects that people throughout the organisation run.

The definition I want to use here is only marginally different from the one you would find in any dictionary...

Definition

Stakeholder: Any individual or group who has an interest in your success.

A very important point to bear in mind with this definition is that "interest in your success" means that they will benefit when you are successful. It also means that they may lose if you are successful – i.e. they have a negative interest. If you are aiming for promotion to your boss' job, your colleagues may have similar aspirations. They have a negative interest in your success because if you get the job, they won't.

For example, you may be aiming to secure funding for your project which will deliver a new product for the Sales Director – who will be a positive stakeholder because they benefit from the delivery of the new product – well, assuming they want it! However, a colleague of yours may be pushing to launch a different product and there is only so much budget to share around all the possible projects and products. If you get the budget, they may struggle. In this case, they are most likely to be a negative stakeholder – and someone who needs to be managed very carefully!

Incidentally, a stakeholder may not realise they are a stakeholder of what you are seeking to achieve, so some of them may need to be educated – but more on that later.

Another distinction is "individual or group". In this process, we usually focus on individuals, but this largely depends on the scale of your goal and the number of people who are involved in the stakeholder management. If you are using the process to get your whole team moving, I'll talk more about using this process with groups at the end of the chapter – for now, let's just focus on individuals.

In this step, you need to pull together a list of people – sorry, stakeholders – who could help you or hinder you. This means people who can have an impact on what you are doing – and this is different from the group of people who are connected or involved in what you are doing.

Naturally, you can easily argue that anyone who is connected could have an impact, which is true but not particularly helpful here. One of my favourite questions when I'm coaching with the *Stakeholder Influence Process* is who will benefit or win when you are successful? Quite often the answer to this is everyone. This is good news; however, to be effective at stakeholder management, you need to get a little more focused while not completely ignoring the masses!

Instead, what you are looking for are those who can have the biggest impact. Those who could stop you dead in your tracks if they wanted to or, on the other side, carry you safely over the finishing line. Most people end up identifying eight to twelve impactful stakeholders – although these numbers often climb with subsequent reviews. If you struggle to come up with eight names, you may need to find a different *Influencing Goal* to focus on (see *Chapter Two*).

One of the biggest risks you have to protect yourself against is failing to manage the right stakeholders. I've found that, generally, people will manage the stakeholders who are most obvious, easiest to access and the ones they have the best relationship with. This is rarely enough.

Stakeholder Categories

To stimulate your stakeholder identification process, here are a few different categories where powerful people could be hiding, waiting for you to engage with them!

Customers/Users

Perhaps a little obvious, but think carefully about this. Who is going to be using the result of your hard work? If you're implementing a new system, the people who will actually be using it are your end customers. They may be impactful themselves, but certainly their bosses will be able to make more of an impact on what you are doing. Similarly, if you're launching a new product, don't forget the people who will actually buy it at the end of the day. Often forgotten with internal projects, but with the rising power of social media their voice may be able to make more of an impact on your project.

Bosses

Again, a little obvious; however, less obvious are the bosses of the bosses; other senior level people elsewhere in the organisation who may be only indirectly connected with your project, but nevertheless could create quite an impact if they chose to.

Workers

These are the people who are doing the actual work within your project. They could be working directly for you, or they could be reporting to another stakeholder. The main thing is that these are the people with whom you are perhaps in most frequent contact, and naturally they can have an impact on what is going on. One caution is that it is easy to overestimate the level of impact they could have on the successful achievement of your goal. Of course, they could refuse to work – but the risk that poses is probably small and the solution is likely to be a relatively easy one, unless they also fall into one of the other categories!

Advisers

These are usually very important people who sit alongside your project advising on all manner of things, such as legal, technical, etc. They could be very important, particularly if they are well thought of throughout the organisation. Sometimes, their advice to the board could kill your project.

Suppliers

Here I am referring to the people who provide their labour, skill or service to help you deliver your project. They are generally outside of the organisation, yet can exert high levels of influence. Consultancy firms sit in this camp and their access to senior levels in your organisation make them very important stakeholders!

Movers and Shakers

You may think that this category is a bit of a wild card, but it is important to consider who these people are. They are the rising stars, the people whose power is rising along with their grade. These could be very important in helping you to really start to move fast. If they can be engaged, can see benefit in what you are doing, then they may be interested in getting involved. That they may also be interested in taking all the glory is also a consideration!

Disrupters

In addition to all of the other categories, there are a whole host of other people who could be affected by what you are aiming to achieve. It is from this group that you need to be ready for the "curved balls" and also where you can build powerful alliances. For example...

- Whose job will change as a result of your success?
- Who will not get the budget they were hoping for?
- Whose job will become more difficult?
- Easier?
- Will your success set a precedent which will make it easier (or harder) for others to follow?
- Who could be jealous of your success?
- Whose power will be disrupted because of the changes you are introducing?

Action

Consider the categories above and assemble a list of names. Don't worry now about the level of impact they could have, just focus on those that immediately come to mind.

Questions to stimulate your thinking...
- Who can have the greatest impact on your success?
- Who are the key people who have influence over lots of other people on your list?
- Who are the biggest beneficiaries?
- Which powerful people could help dramatically if you were able to align your goals?
- Who's going to be really annoyed and is capable of causing you lots of problems?

And a few ideas about the winners...
- When you've succeeded, who is going to be better off?
- Whose life will be easier?
- Whose success will become easier when you've achieved your goal?
- Who are the end users/customers of your goal?
- Who will be able to achieve their own goals much quicker once you've achieved yours?
- Who else will be able to bask in your glory, share in your success?

And let's not forget the losers...
- Who is going to be worse off?
- Whose life will become more difficult?
- Who will have to change what they are doing because you've achieved your goal?
- Whose goal will be unachievable because you've hit your target?
- Who will not get the resources for their own project because everyone is working on yours?
- Who will be embarrassed by your success, perhaps because it shows they are lacking in some way?
- Who are the biggest losers when you are successful?

As you are going through this step, it is important to resist the temptation to restrict your list of names to those who you have access to. Stretch your ambition and note down the really powerful players in the organisation who, if on your side, would be able to make it happen. I'll talk later about how you may be able to engage with them. For now, just make sure to get these people on your list.

Suggestion

If you've got lots of names in any one category, ask yourself who are the most powerful and write them down. If you have categories with no names, think harder or get some help!

The final part of this step is to consider how much impact each person could have – how much could they help or hinder your progress?

In many ways, this is a combination of the benefit (or loss) that they are aware of which could be heading their way and the amount of power/influence they have within the organisation – or more importantly, among your stakeholder group. The more they are likely to win or lose – the more active they will be!

Action

Review your list of names. Mark each one as High, Medium or Low in terms of the impact they could have on your *Influencing Goal.* An estimate is sufficient: go with your gut feeling or get some help.

Use the space on the next page to record their names and if they are likely to help or to hinder you. I'll show you how to do some more analysis on this in a later chapter.

Help	_Hinder_

Hopefully, you have arrived at a list of eight to twelve people. Don't worry if you've got more. If you've got less, you might start to reflect on the usefulness of the goal you are focusing on. If you need to, return to Step 1 and review your thinking.

Working with Groups

If you have a very big goal on your hands which could affect a very large number of people, you should probably start off identifying the stakeholders by groups rather than individuals.

The reason for this is that you will find it very difficult to find the best people to be influencing. When focusing at a group level, you can use Steps 3 and 4 of this process to work out which group (or groups) are most critical to your success. Once you've done that, you can settle on a smaller *Influencing Goal* relating to each specific group. Then start identifying, analysing and mapping out the individuals. Let me give you a little example.

Example

A few years ago, I was working with a group of directors whose challenge was to influence their staff to get fully behind their change programme. On a flip chart, we compiled a list of impactful stakeholders such as suppliers, customers, employees and unions. When we then did the analysis and mapping (Step 3), they realised that the key to shifting the workforce was improving the relationship they had with the union stakeholder group – which to them was a revelation which had eluded them for months. So they settled on a strategy of focusing their efforts on shifting the position of the union (Step 4), which became a subsidiary *Influencing Goal.*

→

→ Three of the directors then huddled and considered who the individuals within the union were; analysed them and mapped their positions. In that process, they discovered a number of small but highly significant actions they could take. Six months later, the HR Director defined this as the moment when the big turnaround for their organisation began. It ultimately helped them to avoid industrial action and build an extremely positive relationship with the union.

As I've said before, this process is not difficult. What makes it difficult is the confusion created by not using the *Stakeholder Influence Process* or something similar to view things at a higher level.

Many other chapters in this book can give you ideas on who the stakeholders with impact are; however, I'd like to add a small note of caution. Don't get lost in the process of identifying stakeholders. Once you've got enough to be working with, get on with it. You can come back later and refine your list, add some more or throw some off. Unless you start taking action, you're frankly missing the point of this exercise!

CHAPTER FIVE

Understanding Conflicting Agendas

Unless you understand someone else's position, ambitions and problems, your influence attempts could be much more difficult. When others don't want to cooperate or are working against you, "conflicting agendas" are often cited as the cause. This seems to signal a barrier to success, an explanation of why you can't get the things done – or is it just an excuse?

A more helpful attitude is that it is simply a question of different priorities. This opens up the possibility that the difference could be negotiated to achieve a win-win situation, while also removing the emotion (well, much of it at least!). You are not in conflict with others – you've just got different priorities at the moment (well, you may be in actual conflict, but often it's a figment of your imagination).

Most of the difficulties arise because of lack of awareness of what the other person has on their list of priorities. Unless you know what they want, how can you negotiate? Until you know what they are trying to "win" you cannot come up with an innovative idea which can enable you both to "win". Instead, you are just guessing – or more likely, just pitching your ideas and hoping they'll be accepted.

Agendas come in two main types, professional and personal. The professional agenda is all the work-related priorities: performance targets, job descriptions, project plans, etc. Some are often visible or easily revealed with a question or two, so easy to work with. More difficult to spot are the subtle influences on the professional agenda. A profit warning can put unseen pressures on key people in the organisation, which may not be openly talked about. Sometimes, the way of teasing this out is to look for the drivers behind the public or professional agenda. You need to dig deeper and look around more corners to see what is really making things happen.

Personal agendas are much more difficult to work out. Items here include career goals, bonus aspirations, or even settling old scores and getting revenge! Without a good relationship with the individual stakeholder, a high degree of intelligent guessing is required. It may mean you have to seek insights from people in your network and consider recent history and behaviour patterns. However, any attention you put towards uncovering the personal agenda will yield big results, because for many people the personal agenda is their key driver. Of course, they will never admit to being driven by personal gain or greed – but there is a bit of that in all of us, isn't there?

Action

Select one of your stakeholders to work on. What do you think their agenda is?

Suggestion

Focus on the most important stakeholder and come back and analyse others when you think it will help unblock an issue or accelerate your progress.

Questions to stimulate your thinking...
- *What things do they tend to focus on?*
- *What are they avoiding?*
- *Who is putting them under pressure and why?*
- *What are their goals and ambitions?*
- *Who are their key customers?*
- *Key suppliers?*
- *What problems are they struggling with right now?*
- *How is their career progressing?*
- *Consider the people who they might view as their stakeholders – how are they doing?*
- *What are they proud of?*
- *Do they struggle to get the resources they need?*
- *What do they enjoy doing the most?*

Use this space below to note down their agenda...

Suggestion

Compare notes with a friend. If they know the individual you are considering, so much the better!

Quite often, I hear clients replying to these questions with a simple "I don't know." Sorry, that's not good enough in my book. Of course it is difficult, that's why so few people do it. But it is extremely important if you want to become proficient at managing your stakeholders.

If you are struggling to determine a stakeholder's agenda, try some of these ideas...

- **Guess.** Yes, that's right, go on, have a guess. You may be surprised how close you might be. Once you've guessed, do some detective work to find out if you are on the right lines.
- **Pretend.** This is not a technique for everyone – but try it before you dismiss it! During a quiet moment when nobody is looking, sit in your chair the way your stakeholder might sit. Imagine you are your stakeholder. What might he/she be thinking about their work? What problems might be playing on their mind? How might they react to different people and why? Go on, give it a go!
- **Ask them.** You never know, they might just tell you. It seems to me that we much prefer to guess than ask. (This does not conflict with my suggestion earlier, because a guess is still better than "I don't know.")

Whatever you are coming up with, even if they have told you specifically, will vary in probability. Clearly, if they have told you and you have a high level of trust between you, it is a high probability that it is correct. The more guessing you are doing, the lower the probability that you are right. Talking to others always increases the accuracy (well, almost always!).

Take a moment now to write down the top priorities (agenda) for the stakeholder you have been thinking about. Try to get at least three in each column. Any spaces should be filled after a bit more detective work!

Professional	Personal
1.	1.
2.	2.
3.	3.
4.	4.
5.	5.

Action

How certain are you? What action can you take over the next week to increase the certainty that you've got it right?

Assuming you have a reasonable feel for their agenda, you can now start to compare it with your own. I'll build on this in the later chapters; but while we're here it is important to remember that in the cut and thrust of organisational life agendas are bound to conflict. This is natural and, in fact, something to be welcomed. Without this dynamic, the organisation as a whole will suffer because the competing agendas stretch the overall performance – survival of the fittest? As I said at the beginning of the chapter, conflict is probably the wrong notion to have here, so let's revert back to priorities.

Action

Pause for a moment and reflect on your answers to the questions below in relation to the stakeholder you've just been analysing...

- How does your agenda compare with theirs?
- What have your agendas got in common?
- What is definitely different about your agendas?
- How can you expect your respective agendas to change over the coming months?
- Could you adapt or reposition your agenda to move closer to your stakeholders?
- Should their agenda change to incorporate yours?

Action

Do your answers to these questions lead you to any actions you can take now to align with this stakeholder? If so – take them!

The insights you are picking up here will be extremely useful in the next step of the *Stakeholder Influence Process*, as you start to analyse the level of interest and agreement they have in what you are seeking to achieve. However, the biggest win comes from the action it inspires to position your plans in their agenda. If you can find creative and innovative ways of helping them to make progress on their agenda while also making progress on your own – you'll be a winner for sure!

CHAPTER SIX

Step 3: Analyse
Map the position of each stakeholder

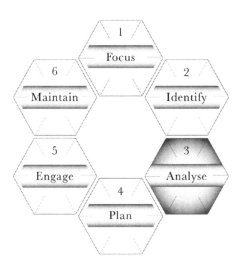

Having a list of stakeholders is a good start; but to get a sense of the priorities, you need to understand their position relative to your *Influencing Goal* and to each other. That way you can begin to see the bigger picture and develop a clear strategy to accelerate towards your goal.

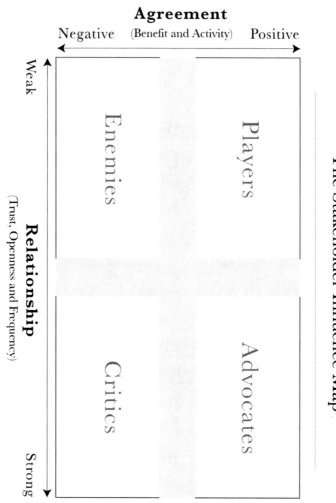

Agreement
Negative (Benefit and Activity) Positive

Weak

Relationship
(Trust, Openness and Frequency)

Enemies

Players

Critics

Advocates

Strong

The Stakeholder Influence Map

Using the *Stakeholder Influence Map* on the previous page, the general idea is that you plot the name of each (impactful) stakeholder based on where you think they are in terms of agreement with your *Influencing Goal* and also the quality of the relationship you have with them (it is the relationship assessment which makes my approach to stakeholder mapping different from most other models).

For each individual, you need to make a quick assessment of where to position them on the map. It is not critical that you have precise answers, sometimes gut feeling is all you can go on. The more you use this technique, the quicker it will become; and as you keep it under review, initial assessments will become more accurate as people start to move around the map.

Relationship Dimension

There are three elements to this aspect which you need to weigh up...

- **Trust.** This is the most important and seeks to determine the extent to which trust exists within the relationship you have with the individual. This is a two-way consideration – do you trust them and do they trust you? Make sure to consider the evidence, as we find that many people distrust others on hearsay or events that happened years ago.

- **Openness.** This reflects the way each party volunteers information. It is one thing to have trust, but this does not necessarily mean that they will go out of their way to warn you when they learn something which could be helpful to you.

- **Frequency.** Both trust and openness can exist in a relationship; but if you haven't seen them for years, the relationship is not going to be terribly helpful for you. If you are regularly chatting with them or dropping by for a coffee, chances are high that the relationship is of the strongest kind.

The stronger each of these elements is in your relationship with the stakeholder, the further to the right you will write their name. Likewise, if these elements are missing or patchy, their name is going to end up heading left! If you're not sure, perhaps because of conflicting evidence, or you don't even have a relationship with them, their name is going to land somewhere in the grey area of the map.

Agreement Dimension

To finish the positioning of your stakeholder, you also need to consider the degree of positive or negative agreement the individual has that you should successfully achieve your goal. Three aspects will help you weigh up where you should position them...

- **Interest.** What will they get when you have successfully achieved your goal? If it will help them to solve some of their problems or make them money, they are going to go nicely into the top half of the map. Alternatively, if you are going to make their life more difficult, or maybe even jeopardise their job or promotion prospects, they will be heading for the bottom half (interest can be negative as well as positive).

- **Agreement.** Do they agree with what you are trying to achieve? If they think that your goal should be achieved, even if they don't personally benefit, then they are likely to be quite helpful and you'll be placing them in the top half. Similarly, they may be in line for benefits, but perhaps they can see a wider and negative impact on the overall organisation, which could mean they disagree. Or perhaps they can see even bigger benefits arising from someone else's project!

- **Activity.** Are they actively supporting you, helping you to clear through the issues and roadblocks? Activity is often an indicator of their agreement and perceived benefit. Of course, they may be very active trying to stop you in your tracks, but not for long we hope.

Depending on the situation you are working on, it may be easier to focus the agreement consideration on your primary goal rather than your *Influencing Goal*. Do whichever feels right, but make sure to be consistent in your approach with all stakeholders so they are all mapped with the same kind of consideration.

A good way to break down and analyse each stakeholder's degree of interest is to use the diagram opposite. The idea here is that this is your assessment of where they stand in terms of benefit – an interesting additional question would be where do you think they would place themselves if asked!

Action

Take the big list of stakeholders whom you identified in Step 3 and see if you can fit them onto the diagram on the next page.

Stakeholder Identification

	Big Winners	Winners	Marginal Win	Marginal Loss	Losers	Big Losers
They know						
Unsure						
They don't know						

The rows are referring to whether or not you think they are aware of the degree to which they are going to win or lose. At risk of confusing things a little, it is entirely possible to have an individual who is a big winner (in your eyes) who knows they may win a little, so he/she could be placed in two boxes. At the end of the day, don't try to stretch this into a precision tool; a basic gut-feeling approach is all that is needed here.

Suggestion

Don't forget to consider their agendas, as described in the previous chapter.

It is on the *Agreement* dimension which you will start to gain real progress if you have been able to be very focused with your goal. If it is crystal clear what you are aiming to achieve, it is much easier to determine if an individual is in agreement with you. Even so, on the first time around the *Stakeholder Influence Process,* you may be unclear as to their position because the greater clarity you achieved earlier in the process was the result of fresh thinking – in which case stakeholders will be landing in between the boxes. It is important to remove as much of the uncertainty as soon as possible, particularly with highly impactful stakeholders.

So, if there is firm evidence that an individual is agreeing that your goal should be achieved, that there are benefits for them and they are actively working on your behalf, write their name in the upper half of the map level with where you have assessed the relationship. Evidence to the contrary means they are likely to land in the bottom half. Similarly, if there is mixed evidence, they'll be in the grey zone.

Suggestion

Challenge your assumptions hard. Many times, people don't trust others based on hearsay, rumour or experiences in the dim and distant past. Where's the hard evidence today?

Understanding the boxes

- **Advocates** are people whom you have a great relationship with, are on your side and really want you to succeed. You are likely to be close to them. Line managers often go here.

- **Critics** are individuals whom you have a good, open relationship with, but are perhaps your devil's advocate. They can see the flaws in what you are trying to achieve. They are great at pressure testing your goals and plans.

- **Players** are people who will agree to do something in a meeting, but then fail to follow through. They say yes and do no. Often the problem is that they are not being straight with you; or perhaps their intention was good, but after the meeting someone else influenced them differently.

- **Enemies** are clearly against you achieving your goal, but you can't quite work out what they will do next to stop you. Loose cannons is another phrase which springs to mind.

Suggestion

If someone is agreeing with you in concept, but disagreeing with you in the wider context, or doesn't think your goal should be achieved right now, leave them in the *Critics* box to keep challenging yourself (and them!).

These titles have been chosen deliberately to be provocative and to stretch your thinking. I regularly hear people in workshops saying things like "to call them an *Enemy* is a bit strong" when they are coaching each other. That's just what I want to hear because in the process the individual is really challenging their thinking hard and avoiding complacency. You would be wise to avoid using these labels when talking to your stakeholders if they are unfamiliar with the *Stakeholder Influence Process.* They will not understand the purpose of these labels and may get a little concerned about the way you are thinking! Just in case, give them a copy of this book and generate greater advocacy!

At least initially, your analysis is only hypothetical. It will guide and stimulate your action. Just because you pop someone into the *Enemies* box doesn't mean they will stay there on closer inspection, nor that they are your greatest foe and are out to get you! Hopefully, once you understand each other better, they'll quickly shift into another box.

Action

Okay, now put the names in the boxes, or between the boxes. As you are doing this, take your time to consider why you are positioning them where you are.

Stimulation Questions...

- What evidence is there that the stakeholder agrees with you?
- What have they done to actively support you lately?
- Exactly what will they lose if you are successful?
- What is it about the relationship that makes you want to put them in that box?
- How strong is the trust between you?
- What can't you trust them with? What can you trust them with?
- Why do they trust you?
- Is the relationship quite open and is contact frequent?

Suggestion

It really helps if you can work through this with a friend who knows a little about your situation; however, this will probably take more than an hour as they will be asking lots of questions to challenge your thinking!

Before closing on this step, there are a few additional things to bear in mind which may be helpful...

1. I've said it before, and I'll say it again – the first mapping needs to be reviewed after you've taken action. You'll learn lots and much will change, so re-evaluate the mapping soon.

2. If you're thinking that one of your stakeholders could fit into two boxes – they can't. They must fit into one box, or between the boxes. If you want to put them into two, it may be a lack of clarity on what you are trying to influence – your *Influencing Goal*.

3. Use a different stakeholder map for each goal you are focusing on. Although the names of your stakeholders could be the same, their position may vary.

4. If, because of your goal, you have been mapping groups rather than individuals, at some stage you may want to generate an additional focus (and a new map) for each specific group you need to influence. That way you can break up the group and look for the opportunities to influence individuals within each group.

5. I cannot tell you how much benefit you will gain from talking this through with a friend, your boss or even your stakeholders. With the clients I have worked with the benefit has been huge – so give it a go when you're ready.

6. Don't agonise over your assessment here – if you find yourself struggling to put pen to paper, do it quickly, take some action and review it later.

7. And one word of caution – be careful where you leave your map!

Finally, please remember that the whole point of this part of the process is to quickly get you thinking about practical actions you can start to take in order to move things forward. Often when I'm challenging someone with their map in front of them, they discover critical new ideas that can accelerate their progress within 10 minutes!

CHAPTER SEVEN

Analysing Risks, Spotting Opportunities

One of the pitfalls of the process is that it focuses on stakeholders. Before you go too far, it is prudent to step back from the people and the detail right in front of you to consider the bigger picture of the organisation in which you want to be successful. This can help avoid traps, counter threats and capitalise on opportunities.

Regardless of the level of skill you exercise, it is always possible that something can go wrong. The severity can range from mildly frustrating to "show stopper" level. The way people handle these events varies greatly. At the opposite end of the spectrum, other things can happen which can dramatically improve your prospects. Often, at first sight they have only a minor connection with what you are engaged in. Being able to spot these and handle them for maximum advantage or, frankly, minimum pain is important.

Ironically, those who get caught out here are often the people with the best execution skills. Their drive to get the result narrows their focus and they can easily lose awareness of what's going on around their project or goal. They easily develop blind spots and miss warning signs because they are so committed (or sold) on the value of their result.

So it is prudent to stop from time to time to look at the risks you may be facing and the opportunities you could make more use of.

The level of detail you need to go into with this is dependent upon the context of your *Influencing Goal* and the complexity in and around it. The more complicated your goal, or the bigger its potential impact on the organisation, the more time and effort need to be invested in considering the risks and opportunities. Even in the simplest of scenarios, I believe that it is worth taking ten minutes to quickly attend to this topic.

There are many different risk management models; however, I like to incorporate the opportunities too. As with the other approaches in this book, it is very simple to use.

Action

Take a few moments to brainstorm all of the key things that could go wrong around your project. What might happen in the wider organisation which could cause your project problems? Then, spend some time considering the opposite; what are all the things that could happen which would really help your progress?

Risk stimulation questions

- What crises could the organisation face in the foreseeable future?
- What critical resources could be withdrawn?
- Is there something that may change in relevant legislation that might affect what you are doing?
- Are there any significant technology considerations which may impede your progress?
- If your project wasn't to proceed, what would quickly take its place?
- If you were the CEO, for what reasons might you kill your project?
- What could happen that would really damage your progress?

Suggestion

I find that it is useful to think of these as "events" which may happen and could bring bad news for you, or good news.

Opportunity stimulation...

- What are all the big exciting projects going on or being contemplated in the organisation at the moment?

- Where is all the executive attention at the moment?
- If one thing were to happen to immediately make your goal easier, what would it be?
- If I gave you one wish (related to your goal), what would it be?
- What event could happen which would really accelerate your progress?

Suggestion

Try to focus on events which could happen. What could come to pass? Even if something is unlikely, it is still worth capturing the thought because its likelihood could change quickly!

Action

After your brainstorming, review your ideas for risks and opportunities and note down in the space below the main ones which you think are worth paying attention to.

Risks	Opportunities
1.	1.
2.	2.
3.	3.
4.	4.
5.	5.

Suggestion

The risks and opportunities you consider here do not have to be outside of your project. If something can happen within it – like some key resource might resign – put it down here so you can think about what to do in case it happens and/or when it happens.

Example

Bruce was aiming to launch a new product and everything looked to be going well. When he did his risk management, he realised that one of his critical resources (actuarial people) would be swallowed up in the preparation for the new EU reporting standard. The business had not yet finalised its response to that change. Realising this, Bruce quickly accelerated the timeline for actuarial input and used his influence to adjust the priorities, so his work was complete before the actuaries disappeared.

Once you have got a provisional list of all your risks and opportunities, you can move on to assessing them on two dimensions – likelihood and impact. It is important to remain focused on your goal when doing this, even though some of the risks and opportunities may be entirely independent of your *Influencing Goal*.

Likelihood

This dimension reflects your opinion on how likely it is that the risk or opportunity will materialise. Although simple in concept, it is a little more tricky when you come down to trying to assess this probability, particularly for those where you have no direct insight or connection. Sometimes, it is necessary at this stage to pause while you get input from other people who have greater knowledge of the situation.

If you are in a big hurry, take a guess and see where it takes you. Then come back later and reassess the position of the risk or opportunity. The information and intelligence you collect in the meantime will help you to become more accurate when assessing the potential impact on your *Influencing Goal*. But if you haven't got it noted down somewhere, there is a significant risk that you'll forget to reassess it!

Impact

At its simplest, this means – how much could each event help or hinder your project or goal? You need to determine the nature of any impact, as well as its severity, and this can become very complex in a short space of time. For significant risks, particularly with high likelihood, this would be an extremely worthwhile endeavour. Unless you really get to grips with what could happen, you could be accused of sticking your head in the sand. Equally, attending to the big opportunities could save you a huge amount of time and energy if they came to pass and you were well positioned to benefit from the event!

Sticking with a practical approach, use your gut feeling to estimate if the impact will be either positive or negative, and how strong that impact will be. As with likelihood, you can seek further input if you need to. Most of the time, however, your first and quick assessment will probably be the most useful and time effective.

Action

For each risk you identified which could affect your goal, make a decision about the level of impact and likelihood – then plot the title on the grid shown on the next page.

Suggestion

This simple approach is not a replacement for more sophisticated approaches, which are an essential part of high-level complex project and programme management. If your organisation insists on those processes – stick to them. The process here is intended to be used more for personal reasons to support your success.

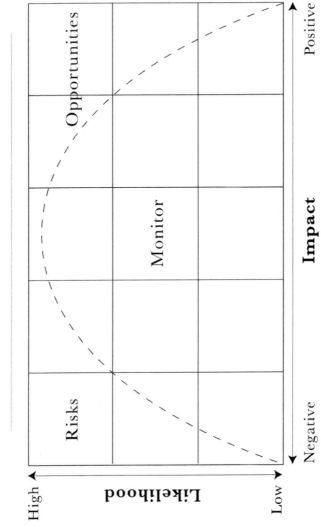

Once you have entered each event on the grid, the bigger picture will start to become clear. You should place a high priority on any risks or opportunities outside of the semi-circle. Those with either high positive or negative impact on your goal which also have a high likelihood of happening are worthy of your attention right now.

Suggestion

Don't get too concerned about the precision: more important is making a decision about any actions you should be taking now to reduce the likelihood of the risks and increase the likelihood of the opportunities. Any action you can conceive to move your project forward needs to become a priority for your work.

The project managers among you will instantly recognise these as mitigating and contingent actions. For everybody else, just remember that my advice here is to stick to a simple approach to making decisions about what you are going to do to increase your risk of success!

Action

For each event you need to do something about, decide what action you are going to take. Indeed, this may result in a whole new *Influencing Goal* and a new application of the *Stakeholder Influence Process!*

Again, I'd like to stress that what I am suggesting here is a light touch risk/opportunity management process. Its primary purpose is to briefly pull you away from the people focus of the *Stakeholder Influence Process.* Viewing your plans from a risk and opportunity perspective may well make your success inevitable.

Example

For some months, Sanjay had been pushing hard for his directors to agree to his expansion plan in South America. In recent weeks, he'd heard in the news about growing political unrest in the area he wanted to move into. This could provide the board with a compelling reason to prevent the expansion which he had worked so hard to establish. The impact was

→

high and from what he'd heard the previous day the likelihood was rising fast. Sanjay decided that he needed to reposition himself and proactively raise his concerns with the board. It would have been easy for him to do nothing; however, the repositioning could increase his credibility with the board and help his long-term success. Although it was a disappointment, greater good could come from a swift change now rather than the embarrassment of being turned down.

CHAPTER EIGHT

Advocates, Critics, Players and Enemies

To become excellent at influencing your stakeholders, you need to learn how to adapt and flex to meet their specific needs. One of the great things about the *Stakeholder Influence Process* is that it analyses their differences, and this makes a real difference to the way you need to engage with them. As it has been said before, we use our labels in this process to provoke thinking and to enable you to take a more effective approach to engagement. Before looking at general approaches to engaging with stakeholders, let's take a deeper look at the major differences between *Advocates, Critics, Players* and *Enemies* and the implications for the way you might engage with them.

Engaging with Advocates

Advocates are your best friends and wise mentors. So give them the time and respect that position deserves. They will be invaluable in helping you to overcome obstacles and help build your understanding of the political reality around your goals and your work. Although they will probably volunteer to solve problems for you, try to resist this. It can be less effective than you may think, and until you learn to stand on your own feet your career may get stuck. It is on *Advocates* that you should ideally focus much of your attention.

Remember that you cannot be complacent with them. Sure, they are already in a good position, but are they really advocating your goal? An *Advocate* will go out of their way to speak up on your behalf. When you're not at the meeting, they will be proactive in protecting your position and promoting your goal. This is different from a supporter, who may stand up for you when prompted.

On the *Stakeholder Influence Map, Advocates* actually sit at the top right of the box. Down towards the bottom left you'll find the supporters. My challenge to you is – how can you move important people up to the far right so they become mobilised, proactive and start using their power to make things happen for you?

An obvious first step is introducing them to your compelling vision, taking them through the benefits they will accumulate when you are successful and consulting with them to find new ways to improve progress on a goal you will both benefit from.

Another thing you can do is to step back from the *Influencing Goal* you are working at and look at the bigger picture of your relationship. The chances are high that if they are advocating one of your goals, they'll also be advocating most of your goals – and you as an individual. In all likelihood, what you have here is a fan. You have trust, the relationship is open and frequent, they like what you are doing and things will be working well between you two. Does this work the other way too? Are you their fan? Do you advocate their work, projects and goals?

In my experience, imbalances are okay, but serious differences usually lead to trouble in the relationship further down the road. If they are a strong fan of you for a few years and then they work out that you consider them to be an idiot, it could get rather difficult between you two! Anything you can do which will improve the balance in your relationship will enhance it and make it stronger – for mutual benefit.

Here are some more ideas on to improve the relationship with *Advocates*...

- **Advocate your *Advocates*.** By proactively promoting others in your network, you are more likely to get the favour returned. They are more likely to treat you well and look after your interests. So look for genuine things you can shout out about.

- **Consider competition.** In the mind of an *Advocate*, who else could they promote instead of you? People are only able to advocate one person or project at any given moment, so whom are you competing with in their portfolio of friends? How can you raise yourself on their radar ahead of the others?

- **Become distinctive.** What is it about you that can raise you in the mind of your *Advocates*? What sets you apart from the crowd? If you can develop your uniqueness and it is something your *Advocate* really values, they are much more likely to be shouting about you. So work on your personal brand and personal power.

- **Add more value.** Make sure and continue to add value to your *Advocates* in the area you want them to promote you in. If you can get yourself into the position of being their resident expert, someone they refer to when they need advice and support, you'll be doing really well. The best way of advancing this is to keep thinking of ways you can enrich your relationship by adding more value.

- **Give feedback.** When someone approaches you as a result of an *Advocate* promoting you, find a time to thank your *Advocate* and let them know what happened. Not only will they appreciate the feeling that they have done something good, but it will also reinforce the behaviour and make it more likely they will do it again. It also gives you another opportunity to boost yourself in their mind.

- **Ask them.** Delicately, but in the right way, let them know what you want and even negotiate with them to speak out on your behalf. This is usually (and sadly) something which seems to be necessary with many bosses who are missing opportunities to stand up and shout out for their staff. They should be doing this; and if they are not, why not? So if there is someone who you believe should be advocating you or your project/goal, go find out why not and see if you can motivate them to change.

Engaging with Critics

The great thing about *Critics* (as we are using the word here) is that you have a good relationship. The only problem is that you don't agree with each other – but at least you can talk about it. And this lies at the heart of the optimum way of engaging with your *Critics* – leveraging the relationship to negotiate agreement. From this you can see that they are not against you, they just disagree with what you are trying to do.

Part of your preparation to engage could involve thinking about what sort of *Critic* they are. To help you work out your best approach, here are the main ones I've come across over the years...

Incidental Critics: These are the helpful people who are generally rooting for you; but on the particular *Influencing*

Goal you are working on, they've got a problem with it. Believe me, this is great news. Why? Because the strength of your relationship will mean that you can quickly get to the bottom of the problem; find out what they think needs to change and then either change it or negotiate. You are dealing with your cards on the table and don't have to guess and assume. Provided you ask, you'll almost certainly get accurate insights which you can work on.

Black Hat Critics: Borrowing from Edward de Bono's Six Thinking Hats, these are the people who are always looking at what is wrong with everything. They have an insatiable appetite for finding fault even in their closest friends – or especially with their closest friends because they care so much! The first step for engaging with a Black Hat *Critic* is adjusting your attitude towards them. They are okay, it's just they may be a little different in their approaches. Genuinely appreciating the value they bring to you and the organisation should then be followed with the realisation that they are doing things that way because they care.

Accidental Critics: These are an organisational anomaly and potentially a wrinkle in the *Stakeholder Influence Process.* These are people who actually agree with your goal in concept, but in the context of the wider organisational agenda they disagree. To illustrate, they may think you have a great new product idea which will make the company successful, but they see it would take a million to develop and that million could be used on someone else's product idea which could make even more profit. Alternatively, they could be agreeing, but now is not the right time because of other issues rolling about the organisation. As with all *Critics*, it is vital to get to the bottom of why they are opposed to you, then you can start working with facts.

So overall, you need to focus on getting a clear understanding of their objections while continuing to build the relationship. The emphasis you place on these two can be guided by where within the box they sit. The more towards the left of the box, the more you need to work on building the relationship.

Suggestion

Make sure you set the right attitude in your mind about *Critics*. They are your friends who want to help. If you disagree with this, perhaps you should put them in one of the other boxes!

Engaging with Players

These are the stakeholders you are never quite sure about. They say one thing (usually they agree with you) and then do another. Their actions don't quite back up their words. What you need to do is dig a little deeper into why they may be doing this, then you can decide on your best approach to engage with them.

Incidentally, *Players* rank behind *Advocates* and *Critics* in terms of general priorities for your time and effort. *Enemies* usually come last in your task list.

So, with one of your *Players* in mind, take a look at the different types of *Player* and see where they fit...

Game Player: These are the office politicians. They enjoy the game and seem to think it is okay to lie, deceive and manipulate others in order to get what they want. At the extreme, they delight in playing these games. *Game Players* tend to focus on small squabbles and deceits. The problem is that these slippery characters are very hard to engage with and need some quite assertive action to put them in their place and keep them away from your work, or at least knowing they can't pull the wool over your eyes. If you have one of these on your hands, take a look at the section on *Managing the Politics* (in *Chapter Eleven*) or dip into the resources for some other great books that will help you deal with the *Game Player*.

Strategic Player: A more advanced and sophisticated version of the *Game Player, Strategic Players* have a bigger agenda they are working towards. It could be that they are carefully positioning themselves and their projects, and to be transparent about how your goal conflicts with them would be disadvantageous to them. Instead, they play their cards close to their chest, waiting for the right moment to play their trump card. Be careful with these, they have a plan and they probably have a stakeholder map too. Pay special attention to the earlier chapters on conflicting agendas and risk management. Work with your *Advocates* (and even your *Enemies*) to gain more political insight into what their plan might be – then decide how best to tackle them. A great question to ponder is what does their stakeholder map look like? A head-on forthright approach is unlikely to work with them because of their skill in martial arts – you'll be on your back before you work out what's happening! So match up to their sophistication and then work on the relationship.

Puppet Player: These are generally well meaning people who are genuinely in agreement, but are permitting other people to pull their strings. It could be that they have other people exerting powerful influence on them, so they genuinely mean that they agree, but for political reasons they are unable to deliver on that agreement. Their masters are able to control their actions. Trouble is, the poor quality of your relationship means that the truth is likely to be well hidden. With these, it is best to try to focus on building friendship within your relationship so they can gradually open up a little more.

Submissive Player: Not everyone likes or can handle conflict. Your impressive ability to assert your views can intimidate people if you are not careful, and some may find your approach insensitive. So rather than face up to you with their disagreement, they may want to avoid raising the issue because it appears to be the more palatable options. Long term we know that it's best to get issues out on the table, but were talking about people here and logic is not as prominent as emotions in stakeholder engagement. If your stakeholder is this type of *Player,* go easy on them. Tone down your assertion and draw them out. Make them feel comfortable and, whatever you do, don't immediately and loudly challenge their disagreement once they do build up the courage to say what's on their mind. You could well be missing out on some valuable insights, so gently encourage them out of their shell.

With all types of *Player,* your focus should be on building the relationship (many more ideas on this in the *Chapter Ten*). Whatever the reason, if they are not being honest and open with you – you'll be left to guess, and I think that you're probably the sort of person who prefers to be straightforward and deal with facts.

Engaging with Enemies

In an earlier chapter, I mentioned that it is often not a good use of your time and energy to engage with *Enemies.* It does not mean to do nothing, but you probably need to err on the side of indirect action rather than engagement. The reason for this is the combination of a poor relationship and open disagreement. When you've put someone in this box, remember that it is usually a provisional assessment and that the title *Enemies* is there to provoke your thinking, not label them as horrible people!

That said, with anyone here you clearly have some big concerns; and if they are powerful people, you will need to do something, and you will need to judge this one well. The general approach forms a mini process which offers no guarantees, but will at least give you a structure to determine what course of action is best for you.

1. Recognise the detail of the problem and become determined to do something rather than avoid or dodge the issue (most of the other chapters in this book can help you here, but particularly the ones about conflicting agendas, understanding power and risk management).

2. Seek wise counsel from your *Advocates* and friends to get their views and ideas about the problem. You can be open with them and get truthful input. They may well also be able to help directly in ways that you cannot.

3. Carefully probe around your *Enemy* to test your theory of what is wrong. Then pull back and give yourself time to consider your options.

4. Consider ideas which could reduce the negative impact they could have on your goal or the likelihood that they will be successful.

5. Are there any opportunities available for you to build a better relationship with them? Many *Enemies* are actually people who don't know you very well or understand what you are trying to achieve. Letting them get to know you at

a personal level can make a remarkable difference, so it is worth a go.

6. What can you change about your proposal which could shift the basis of their disagreement? If you can remove rational disagreement, that just leaves irrational disagreement – and nobody likes to appear irrational.

7. Having considered these ideas, what's your plan? Make sure you have a *Plan B* too and be ready to change course if things start to get worse. Test out your thinking with your *Advocates*.

8. Keep your *Advocates* in the picture so they are ready to help spontaneously when they can. If they know you are about to go and ruffle a few feathers, they can be ready for an expected counter at the next board meeting and stop the counter-attack dead in its tracks. If they don't know what actions you are taking, they may be unprepared and miss an opportunity to stop it.

Suggestion

Military commanders assess their opponents; consider their options and develop their tactics before they engage with the enemy – unless they are stupid and/or have a death wish.

And finally, be realistic with your hopes for engaging with *Enemies.* They always present challenges, and remember that if you are able to counter their negative impact with the help of your *Advocates,* that is often not only the most likely strategy for success, but also the least stressful. You would also be well advised to be graceful and kind when you succeed. Beating an *Enemy* can make them more determined next time – so tone down your victory parade!

Proceed with caution, but smile; you're at the cutting edge of organisational performance. If you can turn an *Enemy* into an *Advocate,* your level of skill will be something to be proud of. If you can do this without bloodshed – awesome!

In closing, please remember that people move between the boxes for a number of reasons. They could shift because you made a mistake in your assessment, your engagement campaign works, something changes elsewhere in the organisation, or maybe they just reassess your goal and think it is worth backing. You cannot assume that these changes will always be positive, but you must stay on top of all these changes as you go. That is why the *Stakeholder Influence Process* includes regular reviews.

CHAPTER NINE

Step 4: Plan
Decide your strategy for increasing buy-in

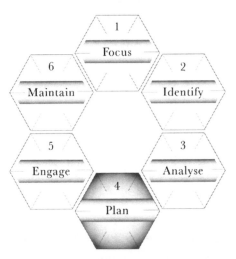

Assuming you have been diligent in your application of the preceding steps – now is the time to pull it all together and make quick decisions about what you need to do in order to maximise your progress towards the goal.

The word "strategy" seems to be used everywhere in business today. Put simply, what I mean when I use this word is the general direction or steps you are going to take over a period of time in order to achieve your *Influencing Goal*. It might be helpful to think of this in terms of the stepping-stones that you need to move safely across from where you are today to where you want to be tomorrow.

Many of the stepping-stones will require a number of actions to accomplish. Some of them may be so important that you may decide to invoke the full *Stakeholder Influence Process* to achieve them, as you move towards your goal.

Another feature of the path in front of you is that it may not be a linear sequence of events. Sometimes, you will need to move forward on many different fronts in the same way that a military commander might fight a battle. At other times, different steps will need to be completed before you can progress to the next.

The output from this step could be called your "campaign" of influence. Using the word campaign helps to position this step in your mind in much the same way that a political candidate may develop their strategy to become an elected representative. This is a helpful mental image because it will encourage you to stay focused on the main task in hand – influencing people. In the majority of cases, it is of critical importance to your *Influencing Goal* that you win hearts and minds. Of course, you also need to get your facts straight and plans agreed; but usually, when using the *Stakeholder Influence Process,* the main job is getting people to buy into your ideas, concepts, vision, etc.

Suggestion

Don't get hung up on the semantics. Stick with the idea that in this step you need to determine the main stepping-stones which will help you to achieve your *Influencing Goal*, or at least make a significant next step towards it.

This step brings together all of the previous steps to look for things you can do which might have escaped your attention before. As a coach, I sometimes struggle to get people to give this element the attention it deserves. Usually, the preceding steps have been so illuminating that they are literally bursting with ideas of what they can do to move things forward.

And since most of my clients are rather fast moving, sometimes it feels like I've got to pin them to the chair to pause a little longer, to take stock, consider the bigger picture, and find the most effective stepping-stones to aim for. If you're still reading, I'll give you full marks and promise you that your diligence and attention to detail will be fully rewarded. If you're not that way inclined, you probably won't even be reading this sentence!

General principles

To keep the bigger picture firmly in mind, you need to start this step by taking a look at your completed *Stakeholder Influence Map*. From this you can consider the themes and opportunities which could be of critical importance to driving forward your *Influencing Goal*.

At a high level, to accomplish your goal, you need to be able to shift sufficient power/impact into the *Advocates* box. Once this box has sufficient power within it, you should be able to start relaxing – even if there are still powerful forces against you, your friends should be able to help you win through. In real life, it is usually difficult to achieve this, but it does form a basic principle – you need to be moving powerful people to the right and upwards. Problems and issues usually lie in the opposite corner around your *Enemies.*

In essence, this means you need to be continually looking to build good working relationships with your stakeholders, while at the same time increasing the level of agreement that exists for what you want to achieve. The next two chapters are worth reading before you swing into action, because they contain a great deal more input into how to shift stakeholders on each of these dimensions.

As you think about the bigger picture and look for ideas about the most effective stepping-stones to achieve your goal, bear in mind these points...

Concentrate on impact: Focus on those who can have the greatest influence on what you want to make happen – the people who can help or hinder in a big way. There is no point spending time and energy on the minor players unless they are your only route through to the real power brokers.

Shift the greys: Stakeholders that ended up in between the main boxes – perhaps because you don't know them very well – need to be moved fast, especially if they are very powerful. It is much better to be sure that you have a powerful *Critic* rather than to be lost in the dark. Once they are in the box, then you can work out how to engage with them.

Move up and right: As mentioned above, the general principle is moving people vertically up the agreement dimension and horizontally right along the relationship dimension.

Movements inside the boxes: Consider opportunities to move people within their box. Moving a powerful *Critic* from the very bottom of their box to the top half may be sufficient for your purposes. By way of illustration, you might imagine that a *Critic* could have ten reasons why they believe you should not succeed with your proposal. If you can win them over on eight out of the ten, they might be happy to just let you pass through. Similarly, an *Advocate* who is in the bottom left of their box could be quite easy to move upwards and right. Remember that the higher somebody moves up on the map, the more action they will be prepared to take to help you. An *Advocate* in the bottom left is often an opportunity missed.

Advocates are top priority: This is often overlooked when considering influencing strategies, because they are already on side and thus don't need to be influenced. In addition to finding ways to get them to take more action, you can also work to direct their action towards specific individuals in the other boxes. They will have different relationships with these individuals, and they may be able to exert more power to remove problems that you are facing. The other great thing about *Advocates* is that, because you have an excellent relationship with them, they will be able to offer you honest and practical advice to help you overcome the challenges that you face. Make full use of these powerful friends!

Critics make great opponents: Because you have a good relationship with people in the *Critics* box, this means you can potentially negotiate with them. It also means that you both have a transparent way of transacting business – in fact, you probably both know exactly where you stand on the goal in question. I often refer to *Critics* as "best friends", because they will help make your proposals and ideas more robust and successful. There is nothing wrong with having opposition, as it will push you to be your best.

Suggestion

I often cheekily suggest that if you haven't got any *Critics*, you are not trying hard enough. Any idea which is capable of breaking new ground or stretching the organisation will have opposition. If you think you are trying hard, just be careful that you are not deluded, because the opposition could be just around the corner!

Ignore your Enemies: You need to be careful with this one and I realise that I am arguing against the famous maxim "Keep your friends close and your enemies closer." In my experience of working with people using the *Stakeholder Influence Process, Enemies* are often the first place for them to focus – but also the most costly in terms of time, effort, energy and stress! The problem is that since you have recognised the poor quality of your relationship with them, and you are correct in your assessment, your potential to shift the relationship to the other side of the map is limited. I am not saying don't try, instead be careful you don't place too much emphasis on these troublesome characters. Far better would be to favour your *Advocates* and enlist their support in minimising the risk/damage that *Enemies* could cause. It is sometimes amusing to observe that *Enemies* often voluntarily move on the map if they feel they are being ignored.

Remember the indirect routes: Sometimes the most effective influence is created through other people. Often the people you may not have direct access to are the key stakeholders whom you need to agree to your *Influencing Goal*. In which case, look for others who can do this for you – enlist their help and support – make them *Advocates!*

Suggestion

Most people tend to take their *Advocates* for granted. Invest a little time with them to advance their activity on your behalf.

Suggestion

Don't get distracted by what is possible at this stage. Now is not the time for judgement – now is the time for clear thinking about what you need to make happen. We'll look at how to achieve this later.

Okay, bearing these principles in mind, let's start to get you thinking about what your strategy needs to be – at least initially. Remember to stay focused on your chosen *Influencing Goal*.

Action

See if you can answer all of the questions below.
If you can get a friend to challenge you with these
questions, it will help you greatly – even if they
know nothing about your situation.

Questions to explore the bigger picture...

- What is the balance like between the power of your *Advocates* and the other boxes?
- Who are the most important people in the grey areas? Why are they there?
- What are the main themes around agreement and disagreement among your stakeholders?
- Are there other organisational influences holding them back?
- What attitudes (among your stakeholders) are really getting in the way?
- How are the people on your map connected (or disconnected)?
- Are there any formal/informal groups involved?
- What don't you know which, if you did know, could help you?
- Who can help you to fill these gaps?

- Who is missing from your map that could really help (either directly or indirectly)?
- What are the main changes you need to focus on?

Hopefully, if you've taken your time answering these questions, you will have been able to begin to piece together a strategy. It is important to focus on the stepping-stones which will be the biggest help to you. So take a short break, get some fresh air and then come back for the final lap.

Action

Try to pull together the thread of your thinking into a few key things which you need to accomplish to maximise your progress on the *Influencing Goal* in question. This then becomes your headline strategy – which you can write down on the page opposite.

Questions to finalise your strategy...
- What are the key things you need to change on your map?
- What priority would you give them in terms of both the impact and the change on your progress and also which is the easiest to achieve?

- Okay, what one thing could you change which would have a dramatic positive impact on your success?

Of course, you may need to consult with others when you are working out what direction to take, but don't take too long about it – you can always adjust your trajectory later as you learn more. To reiterate, the most critical part of the process is getting moving and taking action.

Suggestion

Some of your strategic headlines may be sufficiently sizeable to turn into *Influencing Goals* and using the *Stakeholder Influence Process* on them in their own right.

Example

Sue wanted to bring in a new stock ordering process. It was expected to yield big benefits, but she was struggling to get it moving forward positively. When she mapped out her stakeholders and considered what her strategy should be, she realised that many of the *Players* were also Area Sales Managers. Given their power, she realised she needed to focus her effort on the belief that if she could win them over, everyone else would fall into line. Her headline campaign strategy became...

1. Get invited to the next ASM meeting.
2. Build a communication pack focusing on how the process would lead to greater sales.
3. Influence the IT people to change the process in order to make it more sales friendly.
4. Become a champion for the sales teams.

Example

Leroy's *Influencing Goal* was to get the business leaders to really buy into the benefit his change team could bring to the organisation. He realised that some were *Advocates*, while most were opposing, mainly on account that they viewed his work as excessively bureaucratic and got in the way of the real work. He noticed that one of the *Critics* – Bill – was fairly new to the business and was less powerful than the other leaders, but very ambitious. Leroy's strategy became…

1. Get Bill to recognise how working more closely with the change team could not only help his business, but also help him to become successful and powerful within the organisation.
2. Then, advocate Bill at every opportunity to senior management, pointing out his successes linked with adopting change management approaches.
3. Influence Peter, the MD, to become more active as an *Advocate* and to highlight the causes of Bill's success (process improvement) to the other leaders on his team.

CHAPTER TEN

Creating Stronger Relationships

This relationship aspect of the *Stakeholder Influence Process* sets it apart from most other approaches to stakeholder management. If you accept that influence is a very human (psychological) and social (human to human) phenomenon, relationships will have to figure highly in your priorities.

When I introduced this dimension in *Chapter Six,* I asked you to assess the level of trust, openness and frequency of contact with each stakeholder. That is sufficient for the map; but if you want to find out how to build stronger relationships, a deeper look will be necessary – and this is particularly important if you are wishing to improve the position of *Players* and *Enemies.*

Over the last few years, I have been working with organisations to help them to develop their relationships with suppliers and other strategic partners. For this, we researched the characteristics of highly successful (and not so successful) alliances and partnerships. We noticed three key themes which were symptomatic of excellent relationships. Happily, these themes easily translate into individual relationships too, and it is therefore worth taking a look as part of your implementation of the *Stakeholder Influence Process.*

The great news is that they are pretty easy to understand and also to take action on – you don't need to go into mediation to take big strides on these themes!

1. **Trust and Credibility:** The confidence that you can rely on each other to match delivery with expectations at both a personal and a professional level.

2. **Communication and Influence:** The confidence that everyone is able to clearly state their views, opinions and ideas with an equal opportunity to influence each other.

3. **Problem Solving and Conflict Resolution:** The willingness and ability to face the difficult issues and work to move things forward in a proactive and constructive manner.

If you have an abundance of these in your individual stakeholder relationships, you're also likely to have openness and frequent contact. So let's go into a little more detail at the sort of things which you might notice happening that indicates that you've got each of these in place, and what you would observe if you haven't.

Trust and Credibility

These two words go hand in hand. If you think someone is credible – for whatever reason – you are likely to trust them. Credibility is the culmination of a wide range of factors which build the overall impression in the mind of the observer, including qualifications, competence, reputation and performance. When experienced, it is self-reinforcing and ultimately enhances the predictability of the individual concerned – it builds trust.

Positive Indicators: Each party in the relationship is likely to...
- Tell the truth and the whole truth (are open with each other).
- Share sensitive information (even if this could put them at a disadvantage).
- Have no secrets (obviously within commercial boundaries).
- Be predictable and reliable, or even dependable.
- Do what they say they're going to do.
- Give bad news early and avoid "surprises".

Negative indicators include people...
- Being hesitant, cautious and a little suspicious of the other person.
- Lying and withholding information when it is to their personal advantage.

- Misleading others about their real agenda.
- Creating false deadlines, or moving them for their own convenience.
- Asking different people until they get the answer they want to hear.
- Criticising behind each other's backs.
- Providing inaccurate, misleading or false feedback.

Communication and Influence

It is self-evident that communication is an important element of relationships, but the presence of influence may at first sight appear a little unexpected. Usually, that is something we do to others if we are successful, but not something which others do to us. The notion that it is useful for us if other people are able to influence us takes a little thought.

There are two key reasons why I believe this is a good thing. Firstly, if we want to have a mutually beneficial relationship with someone, we will have to accept that they may need to influence us at times. To not accept this is perhaps a little arrogant – can we always be right? If you have a good idea that could help us both to become more successful, I want to hear it even if it's contrary to what I currently believe to be the right course of action. If you are convinced you are right, come on – influence me and let's become more successful together. This maximises the potential benefits for all concerned.

The second reason is that if one side does not feel they can influence the other, they are likely to feel helpless or even powerless. One side of the relationship is dominating the other. If you have the upper hand, of course this will work for you – at least initially. But, as time progresses, the relationship will deteriorate and quickly drag down the levels of trust.

Positive Indicators: Each party in the relationship is likely to...
- Share views and opinions.
- Take time to listen to the other side's views.
- Share a broadly equal sense of power.
- Negotiate fairly in a way that appears more like problem solving.
- Clearly understand the other person's position, concerns and agenda.
- Proactively provide direct feedback – straight talking.

Negative indicators include people...
- Not attempting to influence the other side.
- Misunderstanding requirements, requests and deadlines.
- Demanding compliance from the other side.
- Complying with demands without challenge.
- Dominating the conversation or saying little.
- Escalating issues rather than dealing with them.
- Showing high levels of stress.

Problem Solving and Conflict Resolution

Once pointed out, this theme is an obvious requirement for a successful relationship. I cannot think of any relationship which at some point has not had a few problems which included at least a bit of conflict. If you assume that to be called a relationship there must be at least two people involved, and that each individual will be seeking to influence the other person, there will inevitably be differences of opinion. If these are not handled well (with good *Communication and Influence*), a dispute is likely to appear.

So being able to deal quickly and openly with these disputes becomes a critical element of a successful relationship. I am wise to the argument that if you have a relationship with perfection on the first two themes, you shouldn't need to use problem solving and conflict resolution. But even in perfect relationships (and I am sure some get close), it is always handy to have these capabilities available so you can deal with the worst-case scenario, should it occur.

Positive Indicators: Each party in the relationship is likely to...
- Proactively take the initiative and open talks with the other person.
- Follow a clear process to remedy any issues.
- Accept responsibility for any failings from their own side.
- Want both sides to make the right decision – together.
- Give adequate time for discussion and to resolve any issues.

- Acknowledge and respect the needs and rights of the other person.
- Look for win-win solutions.
- Seek to build constructive ways forward.

Negative indicators include people...
- Not facing up to difficult issues.
- Not returning calls/emails from the other party.
- Taking criticism too personally and getting defensive.
- Having a "tit for tat" attitude.
- Behaving in a belligerent, stubborn or childish manner.
- Avoiding responsibility for their own contribution to the problem.
- Hoping the problem will resolve itself.

Action

Think of a stakeholder relationship you'd like to strengthen. Referring to the indicators above, assess the strength of each theme within the relationship. Score 10 if you think there is exceptionally positive evidence on a theme. Then get input from others who have knowledge of the relationship and see how (and why) they'd score each theme.

The exercise above can be very illuminating in a very short space of time. It can give you some more objective insights, which can focus your attention on the things you need to do to strengthen the specific relationship, and also improve your general approach to working with others. You could also take this a step further. In the Resources section, you can find details about a unique online survey we have built to collect quantitative and qualitative information based around these themes (the Collaboration Survey), which is particularly useful if you are managing a complex relationship with many people working on both sides.

Strengthening Trust and Credibility

The key to strengthening trust is to understand what it is, how it works and what you (and others) do to maximise trust, or bring it crashing down!

Trust is a complex concept which can easily be simplified into the extent to which you can rely upon someone (or something) else. Will they do what you expect them to do? Can you rely on their word? Can you predict what they will do in a given set of circumstances?

There are also various different levels of trust. You may be able to rely upon someone to tell the truth; however, you may not trust them with your life – particularly if their own is also in danger! Similarly, you may trust them not to share sensitive information about you around their network; but will they be able to resist a really tasty piece of gossip?

When you meet someone for the first time, you are both carrying a set of assumptions, experiences and beliefs about trust. Some "trust until proven otherwise", while others "distrust until proven otherwise". Additionally, they will probably have some intelligence about you – what they've heard from friends and their network. Or they may ascribe opinions to you based on stereotypes.

At the start of the relationship, you will both be assessing each other. To what extent can you trust them? They will be doing the same. Healthy development of trust is a progressive test – share something sensitive (but safe) and see what happens. If that feels okay, share a bit more. Each time it works, a higher level of sharing will take place, confidence grows in the relationship and the benefits can start to grow rapidly.

Problems arise when the level of trust is badly out of balance. If one person shares excessive amounts of personal information too soon, the other will become wary because of a fear that they cannot keep anything secret – they are too trusting! Equally, problems can start to emerge if one is safely starting to share sensitive information, but the other one isn't. They begin to wonder, why don't they trust me?

Once an initial working level of trust is established, building more trust involves progressively sharing more and more. This enriches the relationship and helps both parties to gain increasing benefits. However, it is vital to keep working at it and avoid the risk of mistakes causing a problem. The maxim worth remembering is that "trust takes a lifetime to build and a moment to lose".

People who are considered to be "trustable" tend to demonstrate these attitudes and behaviours...

- Have an open mind to the views and opinions of others.
- Show genuine concern for other people.
- Are open about their own position, even if others may not like it.
- Encourage openness and honesty.
- Congratulate and reinforce straight talking.
- Do what they say they are going to do.
- Manage expectations if they realise they cannot meet a commitment.

People who come across as "untrustable" will demonstrate the opposite of all of these. Few people are at either of the extremes, but knowing where you may sit could be very useful as preparation for deciding what you need to do differently.

Action

Explore your experience of trust by thinking of someone who you trust and answering the questions below. Then think of someone who you don't trust and answer the opposite of these questions.

- Why do you trust them?
- What do they do which inspires trust?
- What do you trust them with?
- What don't you trust them with?
- Do they trust you? Why?

Strengthening Communication and Influence

The first thing to appreciate is that by far the best way to improve on this theme is to make sure you have lots of *Trust and Credibility* between both sides of the relationship. The first theme forms an unavoidable prerequisite to successful *Communication and Influence.* Think about it. If you don't trust someone, the more they communicate, the more suspicious you will become. Similarly, it is very difficult to influence someone if they don't trust you (i.e. they are suspicious of your motives). To be blunt, if you haven't got the first theme covered, you will probably be wasting your time trying to strengthen *Communication and Influence.*

Instead, as you work to improve *Trust and Credibility,* add in a few of the ideas below on *Problem Solving and Conflict Resolution.*

Communication is a topic which has received extensive coverage in a host of other books, so I'll keep the communication element of this theme succinct. If you want more insight into the communication side of relationships, I've listed a few of my favourite books in the Resources section.

Ideas about Communication...

- Communication is a message you want someone to receive. People tend to communicate in their own words and not in the words their stakeholder will readily identify with. Speak their language, not yours.

- How will you know they have given the same meaning to the message they received as the one you intended to deliver? Always find ways to check understanding so you can adjust and refine your messages. This establishes a two-way process and can also offer them the opportunity to send their own messages to you.

- Communication is rarely perfect. People always seem to clamour for more, yet don't play their part in consuming the well-intentioned stream of messages. Then they complain of too much communication. Finding the right balance seems to be more of an art than science, but you can tip the scales in the right direction by asking people specifically what they want, when they want it and how they want it.

- Consistent approaches/processes improve consumption because people learn what to expect and where to get it. So if you are producing regular updates about your project, stick to the same format, design and structure.

- A picture paints a thousand words. More people than you may realise think in pictures, or at the least organise knowledge around a picture or diagram.

- You want to communicate to your stakeholder. Perhaps they want to communicate with you too? Think about being a role model and helping them to tailor their approach to match your needs, then turn the tables and find out from them how they would like to consume your messages. This makes effective communication an agenda item in the relationship.

Turning to the subject of influence in these themes, a fundamental point to stress here is that we are looking towards bringing the level of influence into a more even balance between the two sides of the relationship. Never equal – but to a level where each feels they have the ability to get a fair hearing if there is something they feel strongly about, and that the other party will listen, understand and bring this into account when making their final decision. This lies at the heart of healthy collaboration.

One of the big inhibitors of achieving this balance is the subconscious – or at least unspoken – perceptions of power that each side has of the other. As I explained in *Chapter Three,* power provides a potent short cut to influence. One of the side effects of developing great power is that others yield quickly, sometimes too quickly, and without making an attempt to counter-influence because they think it is pointless.

Since the idea here is to build stronger relationships, the relative power of each side, both actual and perceived, can be explored to look for the inequality. This will help you to identify things you can do to adjust the balance (it might be worth taking another look at *Chapter Three* before you move on here).

Try asking yourself (and others if appropriate) who is the most powerful – you or your stakeholder? See if you can also determine why that is the case. Remember to consider a wide range of different types of assets and skills which build up each individual's power. Also, factor in the context in which you are both working. In some situations, very powerful assets are virtually useless. The opposite can also be true. The only power which works independently of context is the type which comes out of the socket in the wall.

The next question builds further. Does your stakeholder perceive this differently from you? It might be helpful to look for evidence of the way they react to your influence attempts and how they attempt to influence you. If they are letting you walk all over them, they clearly believe you are more powerful, even if you don't see it that way.

The type of influencing tactics they use may also give you valuable insight. If they are using *Ingratiation*, *Personal Appeals* and/or *Pressure,* they could be feeling a little powerless right now. The more they use *Consultation* and *Inspiration*, the stronger they'll be feeling (I'll go into these in more detail in the next chapter).

If there is a big imbalance between you in terms of power and influence, something needs to happen to improve the quality of the relationship before it leads to problems. Having said that, I'd put the chances as quite high that if the inequality is big, you've already got problems on your hands!

If you think you are more powerful than your stakeholder, consider these ideas to help them increase their influence with you...

- Share the insights in this chapter with them. Learn together the importance of great relationships. Even at a cursory level, it will help them to understand your motives and approach and build their confidence.
- Encourage them to share their opinions and don't abuse them when they do if you don't like what you hear! You have only one chance to make this idea work, because next time they'll have learned not to believe you and will keep their head down!
- Tone down your references to powerful friends, veiled threats, oodles of charm and charisma. They've already got the message, now is the time to connect with them and stop showing off!
- Check out how you come across. High levels of drive and determination (very powerful skills) are interpreted differently by others. You may think that it is a normal and straight way of operating; others will just find it intimidating. Communication is about tone, expression and a thousand other unspoken signals. I remember one individual in a workshop protesting that he was not highly determined by repeatedly jabbing his finger at the desk between us!
- Boost your regard (demonstrably) for their power assets and skills. Praise them and help them to feel stronger than they currently are. Don't pretend or embellish beyond reason or they will start to wonder what your game is. Appropriately done, this can work wonders for their confidence.

- Let them know when they have successfully influenced you. It is all too easy for highly influential people to miss this opportunity to give this aspect of their relationships a little lift.
- If it is relevant due to the complexity of the *Influencing Goal* you are working towards, consider instituting processes or procedures which facilitate fair involvement for all the parties, particularly when it comes to problem solving; but more on that in a moment.
- Think very carefully before you reject their influence attempts. It may be absolutely the right decision, but remember that it is all too easy for the other side to see rejection and failure. So bear this in mind when you communicate your decisions. If you can help them understand your process, the reasons why, and also thank them for playing a valuable role in pressure testing and challenging, you are much more likely to build a stronger relationship from your powerful position.

And if you're the one who needs to become more influential…

- Do a reality check. When things are not going our way, it is natural to look for something to blame. The actual level of influence you have in the relationship might be good, but for the right reasons it's not working right now. You cannot be right in your views and opinions all the time – can you? So check out with a few wise friends to make sure you are not imagining your lack of power and influence.

- Look more deeply at the power dynamic. Often, powerful people bring along the power that works for them elsewhere. That may not be so useful in the current situation. Likewise, assets and skills that you have which don't normally give you an edge could be more useful here. If you spot opportunities, start to figure out ways to bring attention to the assets which should hold sway.

- Decide the level of influence you must have to make the relationship right for you; how much you would have if you could and how does this compares with the current position. Put another way, what have you got, what do you need, and what would you like to have?. If you can come up with specific examples of recent events to illustrate this, it will help you prepare for the next idea.

- Find a way to raise the subject with your stakeholder. Get it out in the open. They may not realise it's a problem, nor that it could be working against their interests. This is much easier to say than do. Careful consideration of the other topics in this book should help; for instance, the work you have done on understanding their agenda, risk/opportunity management. The creation of a compelling vision and benefits register can also prepare you for engaging them on this issue (more on this in the next chapter). In essence, this idea is about influencing them to allow you to have more influence in the relationship.

- How could you break down the influence element of your work together? Finding different parts that you can apply your influence to. Sometimes the problem comes down to misunderstanding what each side can and should be able to influence, and what it is reasonable to expect each side to influence. For example, if your stakeholder is an external organisation, it will be appropriate for you to influence their response to your service requirements, but another thing altogether will be influencing their decisions on resource allocation or client strategy. You may wish to influence them to put Sarah on your case, but that is probably not realistic nor appropriate provided they deliver the agreed level of service.

- Consider this problem in the context of the wider group of stakeholders around your *Influencing Goal*. Nobody works in isolation, and all are affected by a myriad of powerful others. There could be opportunities for you to leverage off the relationships you have with other stakeholders to increase your influence with the stakeholder you are thinking of right now. Much has been written on the power of group psychology where individuals are hugely influenced by the group around them, even to the point of agreeing with things that are clearly wrong.

This is an important topic and area of relationships which needs to be worked on consistently. There is little room for complacency. It builds on *Trust and Credibility* and, in turn, prepares the way for *Problem Solving and Conflict Resolution*. That is where we can now turn, but a final thought here – if you're no good at communication, I rather doubt you'll be any good at influencing!

Strengthening Problem Solving and Conflict Resolution

Usually, if you have managed to achieve high levels of *Trust and Credibility* and also *Communication and Influence*, this theme will look after itself. So this last section is deliberately brief because I want you to focus on the first two themes to maximise your progress. Once you have strengthened them, you will have a really good stakeholder relationship. All that is needed here are a few supplementary points which build on this strong base and are relevant to this theme – in fact, they assume you already have a great relationship with your stakeholder!

- *Problem Solving and Conflict Resolution* is about cultivating and encouraging a robust attitude, which promotes proactive and objective attention to problems facing either party – hopefully well ahead of them becoming a crisis. It is impossible to avoid issues arising in a relationship, but it is a sin to leave problems lying around to fester.

- Care needs to be taken to avoid ascribing blame to people, making accusations and shaming people who you think have erred. Equally, watch your competitive spirit. While that can be great to add a little banter, if people feel embattled by you going into win mode, they are likely to forget collaboration and see if they can beat you instead!

- Establish clear processes in complex relationships which trigger a more sophisticated approach when a problem or conflict is identified. Normal dialogue and relationship management may be inappropriate when the temperature rises. If both sides can see the trigger, they can both recognise the need to adapt their behaviours and processes to best handle the problem or conflict well.

- Even in straightforward relationships it will help to acknowledge the possibility that the usual flow of the interaction may alter. Agreeing what you would do if a serious disagreement arose can help to make it easier to adopt appropriate methods for dealing with a crisis in the relationship. Without this, there tends to be a lag between the need to change behaviour and the actual change taking place. And in that gap, bad feelings and harm can quickly accumulate. If you see a crisis on the horizon – get ready for it by working together.

- Watch out for the escalation. It is one thing to have a disagreement with someone who you usually get on well with, but if either side gets their superiors involved the whole game starts to change, rapidly. It is legitimate to involve others when a problem arises, but work with your stakeholder to make sure this is done in a way which maximises the chance that you'll both come out with the best answer and the best relationship. How are you both going to escalate this appropriately? A great question for you both to discuss answers to!

- Maintain the warmth of your relationship while working on problems. Just because you disagree doesn't mean you can't have a beer after work – just agree not to talk about the problems back at the office. By the same token, ensure you remember that you are dealing with humans; and where there are humans there are feelings, sensitivities and vulnerabilities. Overly blunt words or direct feedback can easily arouse emotions which could detract from the process of fixing things.

- There is generally nothing wrong with owning up to having made mistakes which contributed to a problem, but it is wrong to avoid responsibility for trying to put things right. Okay, repeatedly making the same mistakes is wrong – keep learning!

- Wherever possible try to depersonalise the problem you are dealing with. That means adopting an objective stance where you can put the person to one side and look at the facts. And that person means you as well as the other guy.

- The point above may help to overcome what I often see as the biggest challenge on *Problem Solving and*

Conflict Resolution – the natural desire for many people to avoid contentious situations. This can be a deep-seated personal defence system which is difficult to shift, and no amount of process and objectivity can completely eradicate it. So recognise its presence if you have it, or if your stakeholder may have this inbuilt caution – forcing them to the table with your assertion is unlikely to be the best way of engaging them.

- Jointly recognise that the problem or conflict has come to an end. It's been concluded. Congratulate each other for prudent behaviour and arriving at a solution (even if you don't think you've won or come out ahead). Draw a line under it and move on. If it was a big conflict with lots of people involved, you might also decide together that it would be good to get the team(s) together to review learning and improve processes, so that next time it is easier and quicker for all concerned.

Action

With a particular stakeholder in mind, what action(s) can you take to increase the presence of each theme to strengthen the relationship? Note your ideas on the next page.

Taking Action

Trust and Credibility?

Communication and Influence?

Problem Solving and Conflict Resolution?

CHAPTER ELEVEN

Step 5: Engage
Adapt your approach to influence your stakeholders

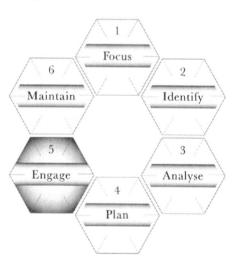

The thinking you have done so far in the process is likely to be useless unless you get active. Careful preparation before you engage your stakeholders will increase the probability that you'll achieve your goal. And this chapter is all about preparation. It explores a wide range of different topics related to engaging with stakeholders. Each of these topics could justify a book in its own right, so what I have tried to do is keep it simple and brief. Where I think it useful, I have also referenced other books which can be found in the Resources section.

One of the temptations with the *Stakeholder Influence Process* is to fly into action as soon as you get the first big flash of inspiration. That may well yield the result you want, but please consider pausing just a moment longer to make a clear decision about how you wish to tackle each individual stakeholder. You have your strategy – who you want to move and where – now you need to develop your engagement approach or plan.

The way you apply the ideas below will vary widely, depending on the *Influencing Goal* you are working on and the stakeholder you need to influence. Some may have no relevance to what you are doing, but do not dismiss them too quickly. Instead, challenge yourself to work out how the idea could be adapted to add value in your situation.

Building a compelling vision

To gain influence, people have to change. An individual has to decide to make the change (albeit an often unconscious process) and this could be with reluctance or willingly. That means they have to be either forced or motivated to do what you want them to do, or think what you want them to think.

If your goal is big enough to warrant it, consider how you are creating a compelling and inspirational vision of the future for people to get excited about. To maximise motivation to change, a vision needs to be...

- **Exciting:** With so many strategies walking the corridors around your organisation, where's the buzz that will make stakeholders sit up and take notice of yours? If you are struggling to get excited about your goal, why would anyone else?
- **Touchable:** Stakeholders are able to almost believe it has arrived. This is a difficult one, but unless people can believe it is capable of being realised, they will be reluctant to put effort into helping making it a reality.
- **Logical:** Not normally a word you might associate with vision, but whatever vision you are putting out it needs to be credible and people need to believe it's a good thing to aim for, i.e. it fits in with everything else, or it's the appropriate way of disrupting the status quo.
- **Beneficial:** Along with stakeholders being able to almost touch your vision, they also need to feel they will fit into the new world and will be a beneficiary. While some altruistic individuals may accept their own demise, they are rather few and far between! And when I say benefit, I really mean that they will benefit more from the realisation of your vision than from any competing visions vying for their attention and buy-in.

Action

Write down your vision in a single page flyer which could be used to get people excited about your goal. Even if you don't use it, the exercise will sharpen up your thinking and inevitably help you to engage in a more visionary way.

If you are finding it difficult to develop a compelling vision, consult more widely about how others imagine what the world would be like with your goal achieved. You can also start to imagine it from other people's perspectives. How might a customer describe the world with your goal achieved? What about other teams within the organisation – how might they describe it to their friends?

Suggestion

Test your vision with a few friends and get their input on how to make it more exciting or compelling. But don't let them discourage you from your ambition!

If you cannot make a big goal compelling to stakeholders, you are likely to be faced with an ongoing struggle to influence and keep influencing them to stay on your side. So invest in some professional help. PR, Marketing or Communications teams could work wonders for you. Most people in large companies only consider using these people for their external customer facing work, but everything they are skilled at can be deployed internally too.

Create a benefits register

If you have been able to get clarity in your own mind on what you are aiming to achieve, you will also have recognised all or most of the benefits you will realise from success. This is natural and to be expected, although it holds within it a risk that you may alienate your stakeholders.

Generally, stakeholders will not be too interested in how you are going to gain; instead, they want to know what they're going to get out of it (yes, just like you do). The degree of emotion and greed varies, but deep down we are all considering the personal impact of our decisions and other people's actions.

At some point in their deliberations, they will also be wondering what you're getting out of the deal. So when you are engaging with a stakeholder, make sure to be clear about what you're going to get rather than leave them to guess or fantasise!

To maximise your prospects of being able to motivate and engage stakeholders, consider carefully all of the benefits which could flow from your achievement for them. This builds a resource of ideas for you, which can be used with different stakeholders as you are influencing them. Although there will be common themes, there will also be wide differences between the motivations and hot buttons for different stakeholders – which is where this resource can come in very useful.

Coming up with benefits that others will gain which may involve a loss for you can also be useful. These can be quite powerful persuaders if used carefully. Show others how much you are putting their own interests ahead of your own. It also demonstrates that you have thought through the impact it will have on them and they are likely to respect this too. But be careful not to push this too far. There is a fine balance between being credible in your care of other people and being perceived as either stupid or suspicious!

Another benefit you could get from this idea is that there may be things about your goal and work plan which could be adjusted and could increase the benefits for others. Often, these changes can be made at little or no cost to you. So, when you're thinking this through, stretch further and look for opportunities to adapt what you are doing in order to increase the benefits for others.

Being open about the gains and losses on both sides of the engagement is most likely to protect you from unhelpful suspicion and also maximise your credibility and influence. And the best way to prepare for this is to create a benefits register in a similar way that you might create an issues log or a risk register in project management.

Action

Draw up a list of all of the benefits which could come from your success. Use the list of stakeholder categories in *Chapter Four* to stimulate your ideas. Put yourself in their shoes for a moment.

Example

A sales manager was struggling to motivate one of her sales people. She kept talking about all the extra commission the guy would earn if he hit his targets. What she missed was that, unlike her, the primary motivator for this salesman wasn't money; it was time with his disabled son. So she adapted her approach to offer him an informal day off if he hit his sales targets and then kept talking to him about that. He got his time off and she got her revenue.

Tailoring your pitch

It is one of the most natural things in the world to be preoccupied with your own ideas and plans. If this spreads into the way you engage with stakeholders, it isn't going to get you very far. It is essential to translate your own ideas and goals into words and phrases that your stakeholder might naturally use, or that will speak to their agenda.

I'm a firm believer in the notion that you should have a consistent vision as the base for all communication with stakeholders. If you don't have this, there is a very real danger that when your stakeholders get together they may start talking about your goal and realise that they are getting different messages. Confusing a group of stakeholders like this is never a good idea and is likely to make you look vague and confused.

These two thoughts may appear like an either/or situation, but there is a very simple way through this dilemma. When you engage with a particular stakeholder, reference your vision and plan quickly and then say, "And what this means for you is..." I'm sure you can think of any number of other linkage statements which you could use. The important thing to notice here is that, because you are making reference to your vision, you are ensuring consistency, and then you are quickly making it relevant and interesting (hopefully) to the stakeholder you are talking to.

Action

Thinking about your goal, consider how you could express the "what this means to you" link for each major stakeholder on your map.

Example

Many years ago, I worked with an ambitious sales manager who was struggling to engage with his Managing Director to get buy-in to his plan to recruit 10 new sales staff. After exploring why he wanted 10, he realised that if it worked, the business could justify another 75 sales people to capitalise on the business potential if the sales penetration rate matched the rest of the business. So he starting talking about his plan to increase the sales force by 50%, with an initial pilot of 10 new ones. He soon had the Managing Director wanting to engage with him!

Preparation for engagement

When considering the action you need to take with a certain stakeholder, one of the most difficult challenges is to overcome your preconceived ideas about why they are resisting, or why they may be difficult to handle. It is vital to be able to move away from your assumptions so you can try new approaches.

The exercise that follows is one which works best when someone else is asking the questions. But if you don't have any *Advocates* or *Critics* handy, asking yourself is okay!

Action

Choose a stakeholder to work on and ask the questions below to help you prepare your engagement approach.

- Why have you placed them where you have on the *Stakeholder Influence Map*?
- What evidence backs up your assessment?
- How does their agenda compare to your own?
- Is their personal agenda likely to affect their agreement or your relationship with them?
- What makes them powerful?
- How does your power compare to theirs?
- How does your goal increase or decrease their power?
- How will they benefit (or lose) if you are successful?
- How do you know this?
- How are they connected to other stakeholders on your map?
- Who else are they close to who is not on your map?
- Who do they turn to for advice and guidance?
- Should these people be added to your map?
- What types of influence might they be open to?
- What strategies have you tried in the past?
- What happened when you tried this?
- How do you see other people influencing them?

- What approach seems to work best?
- What could you learn from this?
- What are your options for action (ideas you could consider)?

Suggestion

If you have a friend helping you, they don't have to stick to the questions above; ask them to use their intelligence and wander off the script to really challenge your thinking.

You can use this question track for each stakeholder you need to work on. Between each one, make sure to note down your ideas for the action you can take to engage with them. These notes should be just ideas for action at this stage. Later, when you've considered the other stakeholders, you can come back and decide on your priority actions.

Adopting alternative tactics

There has been a great deal of research done over the last few decades on influence, which has yielded some fascinating insights into how to engage with your stakeholders. Cecilia Falbe and her colleagues compiled and researched a range of distinct tactics which are commonly used in the workplace. They then set about considering the likelihood of the tactic being successful. The great thing about their work is that it provides a quick checklist of different approaches you could use, so that you can decide which one fits your purpose best. Provided you are aware of the likely consequences, you can potentially engage much more effectively with the right selection.

- **Inspirational Appeals:** Here you seek commitment to your goals by appealing to your stakeholder's values, ideals and aspirations. This is directly related to the earlier sections of this chapter, as it is the behaviour built on your vision and benefits work. Unless you did that preparation, you are likely to be unconvincing if you try an inspiration appeal.

- **Consultation:** The essence of this tactic is engaging your stakeholder in developing your detailed proposals or plans – before you've made up your own mind. Care is needed to avoid the accusation that you are just going through the motions. A sincere inclusion in your decision-making process is a great tactic to get people onside before you've even started. Or if you have already got moving, this tactic could involve you engaging them in problem solving.

- **Rational Persuasion:** The use of logic and rationality is an extremely popular tactic when dealing with stakeholders, but there are limitations and research has shown that, in actual fact, it is not the tactic most likely to succeed! Yet, in certain situations, it may well be the best option with a particular stakeholder.

- **Ingratiation:** In a nutshell, this tactic is about getting a stakeholder to like you so that they are more likely to agree with you. Of course, we all want to be liked or at least respected, but this specific tactic focuses the main influence attempt on being liked rather than rationality or inspiration.

- **Personal Appeals:** Help! Often referred to as emotional appeals, this is where you might try to call in a favour from a stakeholder, or simply beg them to do it! It plays heavily on the personal relationship, friendship and sense of loyalty.

- **Exchange:** Typified by the phrase "you stratch my back and I'll stratch yours", this is often an open negotiation of terms. In an organisational setting, it could be a bargain struck with a stakeholder that if they support you on your goal, you'll withdraw your objections which are holding back their project. Sometimes these exchanges are implied, with a nod and a wink!

- **Pressure:** Assertion and aggression are effective influencing tactics, but are often criticised as being unfair or wrong. This applies less to assertion, but aggression is to be avoided for most people. The type of pressure applied can also vary; and as it changes, so does the common view of its acceptability. Pressure can include threats, bullying, nagging and public humiliation (either verbal or through email).

- **Legitimating:** This tactic differs from rationality because it seeks agreement and the request fits in with other organisational policies or procedures. There may be good logical reasons for retaining a poor performer, but this tactic uses the legislation as the reason to keep the individual. In many ways, this tactic is borrowing power from other sources.

- **Coalition:** In the research, this tactic is referring the use of others to do your influencing for you. It is important to have other people on your side; however, excessive reliance on their influence is of limited benefit and risky in the long term. Unless you can win unaided, you will always be reliant to some extent on other people's power.

In their results, Falbe and her colleagues reported that the most successful tactics were *Inspirational Appeals* and *Consultation*. Somewhat surprisingly, *Rational Persuasion* languished in the middle in terms of success. Least likely to be successful were *Pressure, Legitimating* and *Coalition*. At first sight, the surprise here is that *Coalition* was in the bottom group. When you go deeper into the research, what becomes clear is that it is the specific use of a confederate to do your influencing for you which is less likely to be successful. It does not mean that you should not build coalitions – these are extremely useful in getting more and more people on the right page and is really what the *Stakeholder Influence Process* is designed to achieve.

Action

For each of your main stakeholders, consider these questions…

- Which of the nine tactics have you tried before?
- Which were most successful for you with that stakeholder?
- Which have you not tried that could be useful?
- What tactics have you seen others use with this stakeholder? What happened?
- Which tactic(s) could you use to influence your stakeholder now?

Remember, there are no hard and fast rules here. What you need to do is adopt a tactic or a range of tactics which have been selected for a particular situation after careful thought. Blundering around with your favourite tactic will not be anywhere near as effective as selecting the right tools for the job in hand.

Adapting your style

The desire to influence other people is a natural part of being human. The way in which you influence – your style – has been established over the years by your experience and learning. Subconsciously, you will have found out what works for you. Yet each individual is different, and people will have found alternative ways to influence. Research we've conducted suggests a number of key principles relevant to influence and style...

1. Individuals differ in their influencing styles.
2. People prefer to be influenced in the way they prefer to influence others.
3. Any difference in style creates a distraction from the content of any communication, and
4. Adapting to remove the distraction creates stronger influence.

The message I want you to consider here is that if you can become more aware of styles and then make clearer decisions about the style you adopt with your stakeholders, you're likely to be more effective with your engagement. The resources section will point you in the direction of more detail on this topic; but for now, here is a summary of the key areas of behaviour we have identified in our research...

- **Determination:** the preference to express clear views, opinions and goals and then drive them towards realisation vs. the preference to consult, accommodate and reach a harmonious solution, direction or view.

- **Tact and Diplomacy:** the preference to sense the feelings, concerns and agendas of other people and respond in a sensitive way vs. the preference to be direct and clear with others so they know where they stand, even if this risks upsetting them.

- **Sociability and Networking:** the preference to use social skills to build a wide and strong network of valuable contacts vs. the preference to focus on the task in hand and to avoid social distraction.

- **Emotional Control:** the preference to remain calm and focused on facts and process vs. the preference to express genuine emotions openly as they happen.

Although we have a psychometric instrument to assess these (The Gautrey Influence Profile is described in the Resources section), you can get a rough feel by considering the extent to which you prefer behaviours which would match the first part of each dimension's description. For instance, how strongly do you favour the use of *social skills to build a wide and strong network of valuable contacts?* Note that avoiding these behaviour leads to the second part of each dimension's description, i.e. *focus on the task in hand and to avoid social distraction.*

Action

Think about each of the dimensions above and give yourself a score out of 15. If you score 15, you'll be strongly in favour of using behaviours which sit behind the first part of each description. If the second part of the statement is you all over, score yourself as 0.

Now comes the interesting part. How does this relate to engaging with your stakeholders? In a nutshell, if your stakeholder would score themselves differently from you, you've probably got some distraction creeping in to your engagement. Let me give you a few examples...

- Highly sociable people love talking, often about themselves and what they did during the weekend. At the other end of the spectrum, they won't be interested and may even resent the barrage of questions which have nothing to do with the task in hand. Their sociable friends will wonder what's wrong with them.

- If you are very calm and controlled, seeing huge emotional displays from others will be disturbing. You'll wish they could leave their feelings out of the debate, yet they will be wondering what you are thinking because they can't see you jumping up and down or banging the desk!

There are many other interesting dynamics at play between these dimensions which we don't have time to explore in detail, but this should be enough to give you some food for thought.

Action

Think of a stakeholder you need to engage and rate them against each of the dimensions (guessing if necessary). How do they differ from you and what implications does this have for the way you engage with them?

Managing the politics

Politics is an inevitable feature of organisational life when you realise that the various definitions all lead to the behaviours people use when they seek to influence. These definitions are neutral when it comes to intent or agenda, so those with the best interests of the organisation at the core of their being will be political, as well as the more Machiavellian characters. The actual difference in the way it plays out is in the level of deceit and damage caused to those around. So unless you work in an organisation where nobody is trying to influence people, you'll need to come to terms with how politics works and how you can engage proactively (and hopefully authentically) so you can protect your *Influencing Goal*.

Time does not permit us to do other than cover the basic principles, but the Resources section will point you to more specific coverage of this specific topic.

To manage the politics, firstly you've got to see it and understand it. Knowing the tactics that people could use or are using is critical before you decide how to respond. In our book *21 Dirty Tricks at Work,* we helped people to come to grips with the reality by exploring tactics such as...

- **Fall Guy / The Patsy:** Assigning projects or tasks that are destined to fail to an expendable manager so that they can be blamed for the failure, and/or to reassign favoured employees away from reputation threatening failure.

- ***Rock and a Hard Place:*** Manipulating people by offering limited or fixed choices, expecting the victim to choose the lesser of two evils.
- ***Tell Me More:*** The tactic of delaying decisions or honest disclosure by requesting more work, research or data which often includes the efforts of others.
- ***My Hands are Tied:*** Pretending to be helpless due to the influence of a higher authority or process, when under the same circumstances, but with a different person, there would be a different outcome; "Sorry, Ben, but the policy is..."

There are many more in the book, and even more in our catalogue, but the important thing to realise is that these are likely to be happening around your stakeholder community in various forms. So try to think about other specific tactics which you see happening. This really helps build awareness and if you want to discuss it with a friend, so much the better!

You may also notice that these are somewhat tactical in nature. If you really want to get to grips with bigger political strategies which people use – or fall into – have a good read of our other book *Political Dilemmas at Work.* In here, you will learn about *Consultants Rule, Home Alone, Power Vacuum* and many more.

Once you've recognised exactly what is going on, the next step is deciding what to do about it. It is a complex subject which requires more than just a few pages to explore, so here are some ideas for you based on my experience of working with people of integrity, and helping them to succeed in highly tense political environments...

- Keep your emotions under control, manage your fear, and look for the facts.
- Consider the big picture.
- Offer ways forward / ways out.
- Put out fires and build bridges.
- Walk in their shoes.
- Take some time to think.
- Look for positive intent.
- Ask them what they want!
- Don't fight every battle.

But whatever you do, don't ignore or avoid reality; otherwise, it will catch you out – and probably at your most vulnerable moment!

So now it is up to you to decide how to engage with each stakeholder. There are no rights or wrongs, just that some approaches are more likely to get the result you want. It is also true that any engagement is probably better than no engagement. My advice to you now is to make some clear decisions about how you can engage, then see what happens and adjust as you go.

CHAPTER TWELVE

Step 6: Maintain
Keep motivated, moving and refreshing

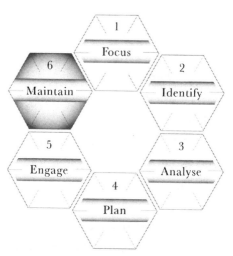

If you want to keep moving towards your goal, you have to keep motivated to do whatever it takes. Few great achievements are accomplished without persistent effort to keep moving forward. And to avoid taking wrong turns, as you move you need to keep refreshing your plans and tactics, learning from experience and adjusting your course. At the same time, you can also attend to keeping your motivation in peak condition.

In this busy life, there are far more things clamouring for your time than you could possible attend to, so you'll need to find a way to make sure that your *Influencing Goal* comes pretty high up the list of priorities. If you have chosen your goal well, this should be fairly easy, but the ideas below can help make sure it stays there – and also that you are able to achieve more than you originally intended.

Increasing Motivation

The main principle here is that you need to find a way to keep going – or perhaps many ways to keep going. If you've got this far in the book, you're already demonstrating motivation; but where will this energy and enthusiasm be in a couple of months' time? When the going gets a little rough, you need to be ready – you need to be at your peak in motivation terms, so that you have the tenacity to stick with it.

Since motivation is such an important factor, you may wonder why it comes at the end of this book. I have presumed that your motivation was high at the beginning, so it wasn't necessary to put it right up front. Now that you're at the end of the book, and hopefully still on a bit of a high, this section can be used as a little preparation for when the times get tougher and your motivation wanes.

One way to do this is to keep the personal benefits that success will bring to you, and also the negative consequences or losses you will incur if you fail at the forefront of your mind. Some people tend to be more motivated by the gains they could make, others by the losses. In psychology, this is often referred to as "moving towards" or "moving away" motivation. Whichever you tend towards, that's okay – recognising it will help you to focus your thinking in the next action.

Action

Get out your *Stakeholder Influence Map*. On the back, draw a vertical line down the middle. On the left of this line, write down everything you will gain from achieving your *Influencing Goal*. On the right, note everything you could lose if you fail. Refer to this often, but especially whenever you are doing a progress review of the *Stakeholder Influence Process*.

Stimulation questions...
- How will it contribute to your bonus, pay review?
- Will it improve your career? How?
- Does success with this goal raise your profile?

- Will it make life easier for you? How will others you care about benefit?
- What problems will it solve for you?
- How will it improve the way your colleagues think about you?
- What new connections/friends will you make?
- Will it improve your personal life?

More stimulation questions...
- What will you lose if you fail?
- How will your reputation be damaged?
- Will others think you have let them down?
- Could you get fired, rejected for promotion?
- How will more senior colleagues think about your failure?
- Will you have enough excuses to get away with it? Will anybody buy them?
- What will your partner or friends think?

This is very similar to the suggestion in *Chapter Eleven,* where I recommended compiling a benefits register. This time it's personal!

Suggestion

Work with the set of questions above which you feel will help you the most based on your preference to move towards or away from things.

Thinking about the gains and losses for an *Influencing Goal* is great, but to be realistic you also need to factor in all of the other projects you have on the go. Your current goal may have lots of potential benefits, what about goal B or even goal C? Perhaps goal A is worth ditching in favour of goal B. Only you can decide, but decide you must.

Action

On a sheet of paper, draw a column for each major goal you are working on. In the top half of each column, write down the main benefit for you and, in the bottom half, the main pitfalls of failing to achieve the goal. Seeing these side-by-side will help you to reassess and refresh your priorities.

Suggestion

If you decide to de-prioritise a goal, remember to
keep your stakeholders informed and manage their
expectations – they may have a different view of
the priorities.

So far so good?

Now, how about raising the stakes a little more? They
say that fortune favours the brave, so consider these ideas
to increase your commitment and motivation, or even fear if
that's what gets you going!

- Have a bet with a competing project manager that
  you will win the resources/get the budget/be first to
  complete.
- Make public statements about the deadlines you
  have set.
- Strike a bargain with one of your stakeholders; with
  consequences if you fail to deliver (you could have a
  bit of fun with this too!).
- Use every opportunity to stress just how critical your
  goal is to the success of the business (careful now).
- Get your project on the radar for the compliance/
  governance committee.
- Talk up the consequences of failure for the organisation
  and everybody who works there.

- Tell your boss you will resign if you fail. (Getting nervous?)
- Find ways to boast to your friends about how important your project is.

Suggestion

Be careful you don't back yourself into a corner and become too personally attached to your goal. At some stage in your regular reviews, you may conclude that you need to force the closure of your own project.

Okay, I will confess, some of these suggestions may be a bit provocative, but that's my job. You need to carefully consider all options which could keep yourself on the move because that has serious (positive) consequences for you and your career.

Suggestion

Be careful not to alienate your colleagues (and friends) and err on the side of light-hearted banter, etc. Have a bit of fun with them if it is appropriate.

A final idea about motivation for you is to use your stakeholders to keep you motivated, either *Advocates* or *Enemies* can be quite useful to you here. By reminding your *Advocates* of the benefits they will accrue, you can enlist their guidance on how to keep you moving forward. Perhaps they could exert a little discipline or regularly ask for updates. On the other hand, reminding yourself of all that your *Enemies* could gain from your downfall could give you just the boost you need!

Regular Review and Refreshment

The *Stakeholder Influence Process* is not a one-off event. It should be reviewed and refreshed regularly until you have achieved your goal, or the goal is no longer critical for your valuable time and attention.

There are two main ways to do a review...

- *A Key Question Review* where you review your progress, learning, and decide what to do next, or

- *A Process Step Review* where you take a fresh look at one of the steps in the process to find creative new opportunities for advancing your goal.

Suggestion

Whichever review you do, make sure to have a copy of your *Stakeholder Influence Map* in front of you, or better still on the wall so the whole team can see it!

Each type of review requires a slightly different frame of mind; so if you are tempted to do them both in a single session, try to put a clear structure in place, otherwise you are likely to lose momentum and wander around the topics more than you need to do. Do the *Key Question Review* part first, then stop, take a break and then do the *Process Step Review.* At the end of the session, pull together your ideas from both types of review when deciding how to refresh your strategy or refocus your action.

Suggestion

When combining both reviews, set an even time limit for both, perhaps 15 minutes each. Be strict when the time is up!

Key Question Review

Here you focus on what has been happening, what you have been learning and what you need to do differently to accelerate progress during the next period of implementation. These questions will quickly help you to find new ways to boost your progress...

1. What progress have you made?
2. What has changed?
3. What have you learned?
4. What action can you take now?
5. When will you review again?

You should also stop and consider if you are actually focusing on the areas which will give you the greatest progress. Remember Pareto and his 80/20 rule – 80% of your results come from 20% of your efforts (and sadly, the opposite is also true). So keep challenging yourself to look for the 20%, which will give you the greatest progress towards your goal.

Process Step Review

For this type of review, remind yourself of the steps in the process of *Stakeholder Influence Process* and choose one step to focus your review on. It could be that you notice one step which is causing you problems in your progress, or could hold strong opportunities for rapid acceleration. If so, focus your review there by reminding yourself of the key points in the relevant chapter, but also considering the points made below specific to the step under review.

Here are the other steps in the *Stakeholder Influence Process* with additional ideas pertinent to the review process...

Step 1 − Focus: *Assess your priorities and focus your Influencing Goal*

After a period of implementation, you may start to realise that the goal you have chosen, or the way you have articulated it, is not as helpful as it could be. Just because last week you thought it was the right thing to shoot for, it doesn't mean that it has to stay that way. If during the week you have discovered new intelligence in the political side of your organisation, it may be an extremely wise decision to amend your goal. For instance, if you have discovered that the most powerful person in the organisation is going to lose out heavily if you achieve your goal, it would be almost mad to continue pushing for it!

More likely, you could have discovered that a key stakeholder is working on something similar. If you re-position the wording and the direction of your goal to align more strongly with theirs, you are likely to be able to ride on the back of their influence, as well as help them to move forward with their goal, thereby creating coalitions and allies.

Step 2 – Identify: *Work out which stakeholders can have the biggest impact*

It is surprising how quickly your knowledge of the organisation will improve once you get going with the *Stakeholder Influence Process.* Once people have grasped the concepts of organisational power, they start to look out on a different world, noticing things which before would have been insignificant to them. If you are including other close associates in the learning progress too, the pooling of your intelligence will magnify this learning even more.

Consequently, there are often significant changes in the stakeholders named on the map during the first couple of cycles of the process. That's okay and natural. Each time, you will be getting more effective and closer to hitting the right buttons to achieve your goal.

Step 3 – Analyse: *Map the position of each stakeholder*

Given that the actual purpose of the *Stakeholder Influence Process* is to shift sufficient power and impact into the *Advocates* box so that you achieve your goal, things should be changing here all the time. Expect to redraw the map many times during the pursuit of your goal. They tend to get very untidy quickly and that is not helpful when you are engaging others in your thinking and planning. But be warned, if you haven't got it written down, you probably are not making effective use of the process. So relax your natural attention to neatness and scribble all over them. That you have to redraw them is a great way of reviewing where everyone has moved to in any case.

Step 4 – Plan: *Decide your strategy for increasing buy-in*

Without doubt, one of the most striking things which often occurs during the process is the realisation that you are pushing in the wrong direction. Sometimes you notice new opportunities for collaboration with other projects, or join forces with someone else. At other times, you may be struck by the realisation that you have misinterpreted some of the fundamental aspects of your project and its fit within the context of the organisation.

These insights can come during any step in the first iteration of the *Stakeholder Influence Process,* but it is more usual for them to be exposed during a review.

Step 5 – Engage: *Adapt your approach to influence your stakeholders*

Despite the guidance given elsewhere in this book, and the huge amount of skill you wield, engagement is always a learning or evolving process. It can always be better. If your progress seems to be stuck, chances are high that the problem (and the solution) could lie in the way you are engaging with your stakeholders. If you think this is the case, it is also likely that you will have hit a blind spot, so make sure to get some input from friends, *Advocates* and *Critics.* Because of your good relationship with them, you can easily encourage them to help you see things which you couldn't see before.

In closing this chapter, I cannot stress highly enough the benefit of including others in your deliberations. Nobody is able to see everything, and ambitious people are particularly prone to closing down alternative views as they focus more determination on their goal. If you are working with a team, get them up to speed with the *Stakeholder Influence Process.* Share it with your boss and even your stakeholders. The more people you can include in your thinking, the richer you will become; richer in insight, action and probably financial rewards!

CHAPTER THIRTEEN

Stakeholder Influence Process in One Hour

Any process aiming at influence needs to quickly move towards action. Only through action will you really accelerate your result. You don't need days of learning to figure out how to apply it – you can start right now with this chapter, and then come back later and go deeper into the other chapters to refine and build your practice. If you have been diligently reading through each chapter, this one will summarise all the key points for you so you can get moving – if you haven't done that already!

This chapter contains the absolute minimum to start applying the *Stakeholder Influence Process* to your work. It will guide you through the process and help you to quickly build a strategy which you can then start to implement.

My expectation is that within one hour you will have discovered some new actions that you can take to improve your prospects, increase your chances of success, and start to move towards your goal. As I have said before, this process helps you to find the actions needed, but does not provide the solution to all your problems. After working with thousands of people learning to use the *Stakeholder Influence Process,* I can assure you that what you will almost certainly find is that it helps – big time! All you need to do is apply yourself well over the next hour and you should be ready to make some fast progress.

If this is your first time through the process, try to resist the temptation to wander around the other chapters – keep focused on the steps outlined here.

Firstly, take a quick look at the diagram of the process on the next page to get a visual overview of the whole *Stakeholder Influence Process.* It starts at the top and progresses clockwise through the other steps.

In the next hour, you should be able to speed through to planning your action. Then you can put the book down, go take action and then come back for a review next week.

Step 1 – Focus: *Assess your priorities and focus your Influencing Goal*

The starting point is working out what you want to achieve. Sure, you will have lots of goals, but you need to get focussed in order to gain maximum progress with the *Stakeholder Influence Process.*

The Stakeholder Influence Process

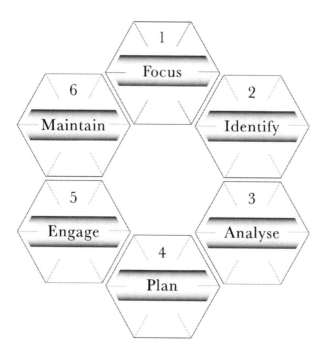

Step 1 – **Focus**: Assess your priorities and focus your Influencing Goal.

Step 2 – **Identify**: Work out which stakeholders can have the biggest impact.

Step 3 – **Analyse**: Map the position of each stakeholder.

Step 4 – **Plan**: Decide your strategy for increasing buy-in.

Step 5 – **Engage**: Adapt your approach to influence your stakeholders.

Step 6 – **Maintain**: Keep the momentum going with regular reviews.

> **Action**
>
> Pause and think of the most important goal you
> have right now.

I am sure you have lots of goals, but which one is most prominent in your mind right now? Settle on one to use over the next hour for your first trip through the *Stakeholder Influence Process*.

> **Action**
>
> To achieve your goal, what have you got to
> influence to maximise the probability that you will
> succeed?

This is often slightly different to your actual goal. If you want to achieve a 5% market share for your product within the next year (your key goal), the most important thing you have to influence could be that the board buys into your strategy and gives you the funding you need. Alternatively, the key influence may be to get the legal team to agree that it is prudent to move forward on the project.

Your answer to this question will establish your *Influencing Goal*, which is orientated towards creating a change of some sort in a defined group of people, or an individual. This will now be your focus for the *Stakeholder Influence Process*.

Suggestion

You'll have lots of things you need to influence for each goal, and likely many different goals. So keep it simple and focus on just one right now, which you think is really important to your progress. Later, you can come back and do the process again for other challenges and goals.

Chapter Two goes into much more detail about focusing your influencing work – take a look when you have a little time on your hands.

Step 2 – Identify: *Work out which stakeholders can have the biggest impact*

Okay, so if that's what you want to influence, what you want to make happen – who can help or hinder your progress toward achieving that influence? Think about all of the powerful people who can have an impact, both for and against. These people will become your stakeholders.

Action

Brainstorm the names of all key people, both close to your goal and those who have a vested interest. Write down a list of eight to twelve people who can have a big impact on your success.

Suggestion

It is vital to stay focused on your *Influencing Goal*. Don't wander off to people like your career stakeholders (unless that is your focus). Instead, keep them all relevant to your goal.

Suggestion

Don't worry if the names you are coming up with are difficult to engage with. If they could have a big impact, put them on the list and worry about how to influence them later.

Although *Chapter Four* is the main place to go to in order to explore this step in more detail, *Chapter Three* will be very useful in stimulating your ideas on who should really be on your list of stakeholders. It explores the fascinating subject of power and how it shapes organisations and the decisions they take.

Step 3 – Analyse: *Map the position of each stakeholder*

Once you've settled on an initial list of eight to twelve people, you can now start to consider their position on the stakeholder map on the next page. Take a look at the map, read the notes that follow, then come back and fill in the names. You can write here in the book, or you can draw it out in your notebook.

Where do you think each of your stakeholders is positioned in these two dimensions?

Relationship

- **Trust:** Do you trust them and do they trust you?
- **Openness:** Would they volunteer information if they thought it could help you even if you didn't ask for it?
- **Frequency:** Do you interact/engage with them often?

Consider these factors and make an initial decision about where they'd land in the horizontal dimension of relationship. If you've got a great relationship with them, they'll be heading toward the right side of the map. However, if you have had some bad experiences, or the evidence is somewhat patchy, maybe they'll fit into the left of the diagram. If you are really unsure, perhaps because you don't know them very well, leave them in the grey zone – that's okay for now.

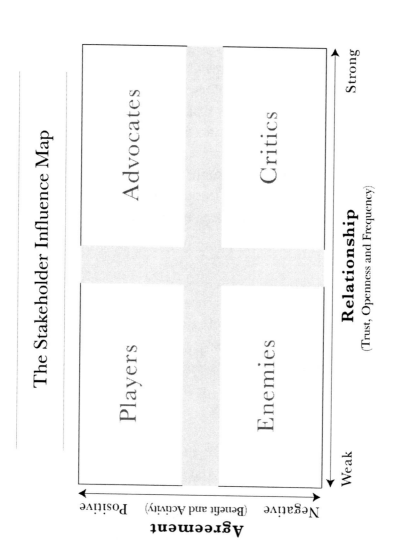

The Stakeholder Influence Map

Agreement

- **Interest:** Will they benefit or lose if you are successful?
- **Agreement:** Do they agree with what you are trying to achieve? They may agree, but still lose out because they know that the organisation as a whole will benefit – yes, these people do exist! The opposite could also be true.
- **Activity:** To what extent are they actively supporting or blocking you? This is often an indicator of the way they are thinking in terms of agreement and/ or interest.

What you need to do is arrive at an initial position for them on the vertical dimension of agreement. If they are clearly in favour of what you are doing, seem to be a beneficiary and have demonstrated their support, they're heading for the top half of the map.

Action

Take each individual stakeholder on your list and write their name in the appropriate position on the map.

Suggestion

Don't agonise over it, think about it and write their name in a box. This will be your initial positioning to review later, maybe after you've taken some action.

You may find it helpful to pause a moment in order to understand the different boxes. The labels are chosen to deliberately provoke good thinking, not to throw accusations about. So to put a little more *meat on the bones...*

- An **Advocate** is a fan. Someone who really believes in what you are doing and is willing to put themselves out to help you succeed.

- *Critics* are people who you trust and will tell you what's on their mind. You will believe what they say. They will honestly point out the flaws in your arguments and will also be open to negotiation. You know where you stand with these people.

- *Players* are the sort of people you never quite know what they really think. They seem to say all the right things, but never seem to follow through. In a meeting, they are likely to agree, but their actions speak louder than words!

- **_Enemies_** – well, okay, in most cases this is pushing it a bit, but generally these are the people who you don't get on well with and are quite happy for you to know that they don't agree with what you are doing. Sadly, they will never quite level with you about what they are going to do to stop you – cause trouble or influence powerful people to remove the funding for your project.

- People in the grey areas are the ones who you are unsure about. Later, you will be taking different actions depending on which boxes they fall between. If they are people with power, they will need to be taken seriously.

Action

Go on, write the names in the boxes – now is not the time for long, drawn-out ruminating – make an initial (if private) commitment to the position of your stakeholders.

Suggestion

Write their names down in pencil if you think you may change your mind – that's okay!

There is much more detail on the things you need to be considering on this step in *Chapter Six*. However, this extra detail is only useful right now if you are really stuck – I would much sooner you have a go and move on to the next step. Leave the deeper immersion in the application of the *Stakeholder Influence Process* for your first review!

Step 4 – Plan: *Decide your strategy for increasing buy-in*

So what do you need to change? When you have placed the impactful stakeholders on your map, you need to start thinking about whom you need to move.

Quite often, there will be one individual who holds the key to bringing all the others around to your way of thinking – or to your opponent's way of thinking. These people may not be the most obvious. In fact, they are often a few steps removed from the distracting cut and thrust – yet they exert massive influence over the way things are moving.

Action

Pause and consider what needs to change to dramatically improve the situation. Try to come up with three key things which need to change.

Questions to stimulate your strategy...

- What one change would create a massive movement towards your goal?
- Who is the key person blocking you right now?
- What core attitudes need to shift to remove all obstacles?
- If you could wave a magic wand and move one stakeholder over to your side – who would that be?

Suggestion

Try to focus on the bigger picture and the things which, if you could change, would have a snowball effect – the things which would sweep away opposition and make success a foregone conclusion!

Chapter Nine will go into more detail if you need it on this step, and *Chapter Seven* on risks and opportunities is also worth taking a look at if you are struggling to come up with an initial strategy to get you moving towards your goal.

In fact, on most occasions when I am taking clients through this stage, they don't need much help beyond the stimulation questions to figure out who they need to be working on.

Suggestion

Your aim is to move sufficiently powerful (impactful) people right and upwards to achieve the influence you desire – and make the accomplishment of your goal a certainty.

Step 5 – Engage: *Adapt your approach to influence your stakeholders*

In *Chapter Eight,* I will go into more detail about how to engage with each type of stakeholder, but you don't need that now. If you are like most of my clients and workshop delegates, the preceding steps will have already opened your eyes to what I often call a "blinding flash", which has been sitting in front of you, begging for attention. So, at this stage, I'll just give you a few pointers...

- Go seek the advice of your *Advocates.* They are your best friends and can (and probably will) give you wise counsel on how to solve the challenges you have elsewhere on your map – particularly with *Enemies*!

- Engage with your *Critics* in a positive attitude. You have a good relationship with them and you can take a negotiating approach with them. The great thing about *Critics* is that they will be honest with you, so you can find out what you need to do to win them over.

- If you need to, aim to build your relationship with *Players.* There is something not quite right about the way you two are working together and communicating. So consider bringing this to the table and – without threatening – see if you can cultivate a more authentic way of doing business together. Alternatively, work with more powerful people!

- Don't fuss too much about your *Enemies.* Of course, you have to do something about really powerful ones, but generally I find that these characters revel in the attention. Instead, work with *Advocates* (and even *Critics*) to minimise the damage these people could do.

Later, when you have time, you can also take a look at *Chapters Ten* and *Eleven* about Engaging Stakeholders and

Strengthening Relationships. But don't worry about that now unless you absolutely have to. Generally, what I find is that once people work out who they need to focus on they also find they are more than capable of making it happen. At risk of appearing dismissive of my eminent colleagues in other disciplines, a healthy dose of common sense doesn't need a liberal amount of theoretical confusion!

Step 6 – Maintain: *Keep motivated, moving and refreshing*

Okay, at this stage this is pretty easy. You're already motivated and moving, so fix a time in your diary to refresh your plans by reviewing your progress. You've got to keep coming back to this process to review how you are doing, what you have learnt and what else you need to do to keep moving towards your goal.

Chapter Twelve will give you more ideas and a few processes for your review, but before you look there – do something first. Take action to start moving faster towards your goal and then take a look at *Chapter Twelve*!

My hope is that this hour has been well spent and you have come up with some great ideas for moving forward your results with greater buy-in from your stakeholders. I also hope that you have been able to get a feel for the potential of the *Stakeholder Influence Process.* It really is quite simple once you've understood the basics, but it is also quite subtle and deeper understanding and continued learning will reward you well.

If you need it, the next chapter will take you through a simple example based on a real client situation. After that, it's just a question of you getting on with using the process and keeping coming back to strengthen your practise!

Suggestion

Your hour must be over now. So get up and start taking action. Fortune may favour the brave, but the brave are nothing if there is no action!

CHAPTER FOURTEEN

Securing Resources for Project Hawaii: An Example

To put a bit more meat on the bone, let's take a quick look at Jim's work as he begins to go through the *Stakeholder Influence Process.* To help you understand how to implement your own version, it is only necessary for us to illustrate here the first four steps in the process. While we could speculate on how to engage and maintain, I don't think this is a valuable use of your time right now.

Project Hawaii is based on a real client, but naturally the names and the situation have been disguised.

Step 1 – Focus: *Assess your priorities and focus your Influencing Goal*

As a busy programme manager, Jim had plenty of things to do. He had five different projects on the go, most of which were going along reasonably well. The one which was worrying him the most was Project Hawaii. The name disguised the boring nature of this attempt to innovate the company's Management Information System. He was struggling to get the resources he needed and some key deadlines were looming.

"If only my sponsor Anne would get a little more active and help me find the resources I need from Finance." This had been occupying quite a bit of time and so far Jim had failed to make any progress on this. He noted down his *Influencing Goal* as...

"Finance will provide 50 hours of suitably qualified resource per month (at least grade C10)."

Suggestion

Influencing Goals can always be specified with greater accuracy, but don't get overly worried about it. Provided it's good enough to get you focused, move on. You can always refine it during a review

Suggestion

Note how he could have set the goal as "Anne will get Finance to…", but this would have been less useful as a focus because it only involves influencing one person (look at *Chapter Two* for more on this).

Step 2 – Identify: *Work out which stakeholders can have the biggest impact*

As Management Services Director and sponsor of Jim's project, Anne was obviously a key stakeholder. Jim also noted down the existing project team members who were also feeling the strain because of the gap in resources. The key ones were Peter, Sanjay and Felicity. Clearly, Marco as the Finance Director could have a big impact – particularly since he was the one currently saying no! After a little more thought, it occurred to him that the people who would benefit most if his project landed was the Managing Director and the two Operations Directors, as they would use the real time data to make their day-to-day decisions as they grew the business – so he added Joe, Dawn and Bernd.

Luckily, Jim was able to chat it through with a close colleague, who asked quite a few challenging questions. One revelation which came from this was that Marco was facing requests for his resource from several other projects too. There were two big ones...

- Firstly, Project Malta run by David would launch a new product onto the market. This project was sponsored by the Marketing Director, Tanja. Rooting for this was Sally, Head of Sales. She was quite active drumming up enthusiasm for this big opportunity.

- Also, a little known project looking at the budgeting process. This had been going on for some time, reporting to the Finance Director. Like many of these types of projects, it was resource hungry and Charlie, the project manager, seemed to be quite good at holding onto the resources he needed.

There were lots of other people, but these seemed to be the main ones who could help or hinder Jim in securing the resources he needed to complete his project on time. In summary, the stakeholders were...

- Anne: Sponsor of Jim's project
- Peter, Sanjay and Felicity: Jim's key project team members
- Marco: Finance Director
- Joe: Managing Director
- Dawn and Bernd: Operations Directors
- Tanja: Marketing Director
- Sally: Head of Sales
- Charlie: Project Manager for Budget Process Control

Step 3 – Analyse: *Map the position of each stakeholder*

What Jim realised when doing the analysis...

1. Although Sanjay was on his own team, Jim noted that he was often making supportive noises, but was repeatedly failing to play his part in pushing for more resource. Jim started to suspect that he could be a little sensitive about his role on the project and may be feeling vulnerable. If a more experienced resource joined the team, Sanjay could feel threatened. It was only a hunch, but there was definitely something not quite right.

2. Anne was an *Advocate,* but that title didn't quite fit. She should be very much in agreement, but why had she not been able to make it happen and get Marco to allocate the necessary resource? They had always got on well and Jim had noticed lately that she seemed a little distracted or at least disinterested in Hawaii.

3. Marco was clearly against giving up his resource, otherwise it would have happened by now, but Jim didn't know him very well. There had never been any trouble or reason to doubt what he said – they'd nod to each other in the corridor, but that was about it.

4. Tanja was a completely different story, who didn't like and get on with her!? However, even behind the smile, it was clear she wanted to get her work done first and had

even joked over a coffee that Jim would just have to wait his turn!

5. Charlie had a fearsome reputation. He was one of those devious characters who seemed to delight in seeing others struggle – it had even been rumoured that he'd gone out of his way last year to embarrass someone on the board for no other reason than to have a bit of fun. He did once try that on Jim, but didn't quite get away with it because the MD (Joe) took him to one side and had one of those little chats which were almost part of company folklore. Of course, Joe was on the same page when it came to Hawaii, but Charlie, no way.

6. Dawn and Bernd were the types that always said the right thing but never really seemed to do anything. Only last week, Dawn had agreed to put pressure on Marco to get the resources sorted out, but nothing had happened – and not for the first time. He had started to think that they were just making the right noises to keep on the right side of Jim and avoid one of those quiet chats.

7. Sally was a bit of an enigma. He couldn't quite figure her out. In fact, he wondered whether she should be on the stakeholder map at all.

On the next page you'll see the map he produced.

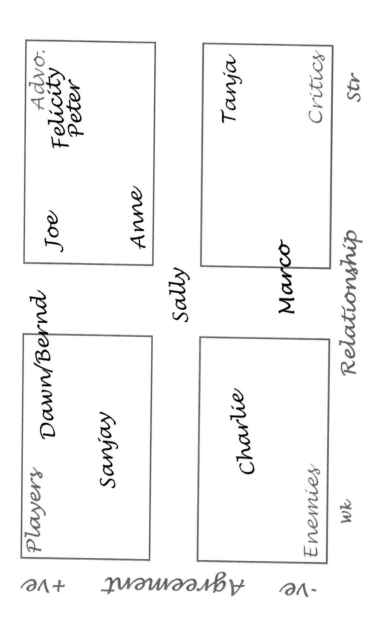

Suggestion

You are more than welcome to write all over one of the maps in the book; however, I much prefer clients to be able to draw a quick one from memory. If someone can't remember how to do this, I know they haven't been maintaining the process!

Step 4 – Plan: *Decide your strategy for increasing buy-in*

To cut a long story short, Jim realised that Sally and Tanja were becoming much more powerful. They had been highly successful lately in working together to bring new products to market and had made the company lots of money. Marco was someone who had been powerful for a long time. But after many rounds of cost cutting and dwindling market share, the others were starting to think that the cuts had been too deep. Last year's budget round had seen the marketing/sales budget rise by 20%, which came as a big surprise to many people around the office.

Jim had not considered the link with sales before – he was really a numbers man and had concentrated on getting the system delivered so the MD could make decisions. Of course, one of the benefits of the system was that sales numbers were easier to get and that could help Sally to adjust her sales strategy and tactics much more quickly. Her traditional approach was gut feeling, which seemed to be doing okay; but if she could back it up with numbers, she'd probably be able to capture even more sales and, subsequently, get an even bigger development budget next year.

So his strategy headlines became...

1. Convince Tanja and Sally of the benefits of having immediate sales data (i.e. move them into the *Advocates* box).

2. Then ask them to help him get the resources he needed from Marco to complete the project and get the system ready for use when they launched their new product.

3. Get closer to Marco and build more of a personal relationship to make things a little warmer.

4. Put in place a standard communication plan to keep all stakeholders up to date on progress, but also regularly reinforce the commercial benefits which would flow from full implementation.

One of the great benefits of the *Stakeholder Influence Process* is its flexibility. It can handle whatever level of detail you want to throw at it. Provided your goal is close to the criteria set out in *Chapter Two,* it should help you move forward. Of course, you can always go deeper, and that is very tempting when you are using the map with other colleagues, but I strongly recommend that you move quickly to action. There is little point in spending hours and hours pursuing the ultimate answer. The only way you can arrive at that is if you have perfect knowledge, and when much of the time we are probing into people's feelings, attitudes and power, personally I think that would be stretching it a bit.

So do it quickly, take some action, and then come back and think some more. Each time you do this, your clarity will improve and you'll find that your understanding will grow very quickly.

CHAPTER FIFTEEN

Modus Operandi

Okay, this is the end, at least for now. I've said all I wanted to say and I hope you've gained from it. In fact, the only other thing I want to say here is to raise a vital topic and one very close to my heart. I want you to embed this in your way of working. I want you to make the *Stakeholder Influence Process* a central part of the way you operate – because I know from experience that the benefits keep building as you continue to use it and apply it to different challenges. So here are a few ideas which I have seen clients use to effectively embed the process and keep it delivering the results.

Challenging Problems

Success which involves the help of others is made easier if you are good at influencing. The opposite is also true.

Whenever you are unsuccessful, take a look at how influential you are being. Try to get into the habit that when things are not going right, when you seem to be hitting brick walls or struggling to move forward – sit back a moment and ponder two questions...

- What do you need to influence to overcome the problem?
- What do you need to influence to succeed?

As you start thinking through the answers, you may be able to spot an opportunity for a new *Influencing Goal* that you can use as the focus for the *Stakeholder Influence Process*. Provided it is a goal which requires change in a number of people, has natural opponents and will take a while to achieve – it would be a good goal to focus the process on. If so, draw out a map and get to work!

Making these two questions pop into your head at the right time comes down to habit. And habits are formed through only one thing – repetition. So find ways to make it a habit, even if this means priming others to keep reminding you too. The next idea explores how this could work.

Performance Reviews, Appraisals and 1:1's

If the process works for you, get others on your team to use it too. If you have people who report to you, introduce them to the process, show them how to use it and then insist that you will use it as a way of working with them.

Once they know how to do it, when they come to you for help with something they are working on, ask them to show you their *Stakeholder Influence Map.* Looking at the map, you can then discuss what they need to influence to achieve their result, which people are in agreement, who they need to build stronger relationships with, etc. It may not be an appropriate technique all of the time, but if they are working on important projects, and they have to work with other people around the business, it will help structure your coaching support.

And in the process of helping them, it will also reinforce the process and its usefulness in your own work too! This leads nicely to the final idea.

Team Process

Some of the biggest benefits I have seen are where a team get together around a table to discuss what they need to make happen (influence) to achieve their goals. Then, at the right moment, the table gets split up into the different boxes of the *Stakeholder Influence Map,* and the discussion turns to the people who can help or hinder, and the relationship the team has with them. This quickly encourages sharing and deep debate with a clear and positive focus towards the team's goal.

In our team workshops, we often use index cards to write the stakeholders' names on. Then one individual puts the card somewhere on the table and talks through their rationale for choosing that position on the map. Team members then start to challenge and the card moves around a bit before settling by common consent. After the high-impact stakeholders have been discussed and positioned, the debate can then move to what needs to change – and how to make it happen.

Using the *Stakeholder Influence Process* in this way builds a common understanding of the problems and issues facing the team. It helps them to understand each other's perspectives, opinions and also their inside knowledge. Often, it emerges that while the team as a whole may have a poor relationship with one stakeholder, one member may have a great relationship. This can be a catalyst for improved appreciation, breaking down barriers and helping the whole team to become more effective. The team member who has the good relationship can then be called into action on behalf of the team and sent off to do some influencing!

With more people around you familiar with the process and the benefits, the more likely it will be that when you are stuck someone else will suggest using the *Stakeholder Influence Process.*

So please, can you now just go do it? Make it work for you and reap the rewards. Come and visit us at The Influence Blog (www.gautreygroup.com/blog) and make sure to keep developing your approach. And don't miss the opportunity to see what we have in the Resources section to boost your performance!

Good luck. If it can work for Mark, it can work for you. Survive and thrive!

Resources

Further Reading

21 Dirty Tricks at Work, Mike Phipps and Colin Gautrey, Capstone Wiley 2005

Political Dilemmas at Work, Dr Gary Ranker, Colin Gautrey and Mike Phipps, John Wiley & Sons 2008

Power, Why Some People Have It-And Others Don't, Jeffrey Pfeffer, Collins Business 2010

Managing With Power: Politics and Influence in Organizations, Jeffrey Pfeffer, Harvard Business School Press 1994

Political Savvy: Systematic Approaches to Leadership Behind the Scenes, Joel R. DeLuca, EBG Publications 1999

Working the Shadow Side: A Guide to Positive Behind the Scenes Management, Gerard Egan, Jossey Bass Wiley, 1994

Influence Without Authority, Allan R. Cohen and David L. Bradford, John Wiley & Sons Inc. 2005

The Inner Game of Work, Timothy W. Gallwey, Villard Books 2000

Emotional Intelligence, Daniel Goleman, Bloomsbury 1996

The 48 Laws of Power, Robert Greene, Profile Books 2000

The Art of Rhetoric, Aristotle, Penguin 1991

Assertiveness at Work, Ken and Kate Back, McGraw Hill 1982

The Gautrey Group

We work with individuals and groups all over the world, helping them to become more influential. With greater influence, careers develop, results are delivered and increased satisfaction is achieved.

We focus exclusively on this area. So, if you want coaching, training or consultancy in how to become more influential, you'll find our insights and methods are world class. Our thought leadership is provided by Colin Gautrey, a widely recognised expert on the practical use of power and influence in the workplace.

Based on the content of this book, you may be interested to learn more about...

The Gautrey Influence Profile

This unique psychometric (referred to in *Chapter Eleven*) helps clients to understand how they prefer to influence, how others may differ, and then make decisions about how to flex their style to become more influential.

The Collaboration Survey

Based on our research into the successes and failures of large-scale relationships, this online feedback tool collects data about the quality of each theme that needs to be strong in any great relationship (see *Chapter Twelve*).

visit

www.advocatesandenemies.com/resources

or

www.advocatesandenemies.com/contact

to find out more

More by Colin Gautrey

Additional titles by Colin are available in several eBook formats. They are short, succinct and get you to the action quickly. So if you like this book, you'll love these eBooks too!

Personal Branding: How to create the right impression while being yourself.

Don't miss out on making the right impression with your stakeholders. It is not about boasting, it is about making deliberate decisions about how you want to come across. Then you can take the simple steps here to start improving your brand among your stakeholders.

www.advocatesandenemies.com/brand

Flexing Your Style: Understanding how to change your behaviour to create more influence.

If you find it difficult to understand your stakeholder, the dimensions of influence could hold the key to unlocking your engagement. Solid research backs up these basic concepts and will help you to figure how to adapt your behaviour for greater influence.

www.advocatesandenemies.com/style

Managing Politics: How to cut through the office politics without getting hurt.

Unless you learn how to engage with the *Players,* you could be missing significant opportunities to advance your goals. You don't have to play games, but you do have to know what is going on and take some simple approaches to turn things around. This will show you how.

www.advocatesandenemies.com/politics

Index

About Colin Gautrey

Colin is a specialist in the practical use of power and influence in the workplace. He combines solid research with deep personal experience in corporate life to offer his clients critical, yet simple insights into how to get results with greater influence.

He learned how to influence in the field. He has worked in many disciplines, including Mergers and Acquisitions, International Strategy, Information Technology, Sales and Leadership Development. After taking a career break from the cut and thrust of corporate life, Colin decided in 2003 to dedicate his time to helping others to become more influential. With a significant level of research and extensive work with clients, Colin has quickly established himself as one of the leading experts in his area.

Along with a significant portfolio of corporate clients, Colin also works with many other organisations, including Warwick Business School, Institute of Directors and The Conference Board.

You will find Colin very approachable, knowledgeable and totally enthusiastic about his subject. Although being recognised as a leading expert in his area, he applies the *"always more to learn"* approach to his work. Colin is available to work with clients anywhere in the world and is skilled at remote working.

If you would like to engage Colin for your conference or to come and work with your people, please get in touch.

www.advocatesandenemies.com/contact

http://twitter.com/colingautrey